Let's
Stir
Some
Thoughts

Giridhar Jaded

ARPress

ARPress
45 Dan Road Suite 36
Canton MA 02021

Hotline: 1(800) 220-7660
Fax: 1(855) 752-6001

Ordering Information:
Quantity sales. Special discounts are available on quantity purchases by corporations, associations, and others. For details, contact the publisher at the address above.

Printed in the United States of America.

ISBN-13:   Paperback   979-8-89389-911-5
           eBook   979-8-89389-912-2

Library of Congress Control Number: 2024923855

Dedication Page

A photo on my living room wall,

Makes the place feel like home,

A picture of two different times,

Made into one for lack of time,

To be captured posing together,

A photo of my Mother & my Father,

Who left me in that very order.

But made me enough of a fighter,

To live a life of kindness, for it matters,

You are with me, without being with me,

You did enough to let me be a better me.

My first book is an offering at your feet,

On a journey new, Mom & Dad, your blessings, all I seek.

Contents

1. Prose versus Poetry 1
2. Twenty-Four hours called life 2
3. Free Books... 3
4. Post card on the wall 4
5. When the tables turn... 5
6. The thoughts that fade 6
7. Shiny twigs... 7
8. Together 8
9. Technology for a cause...................................... 9
10. Mr. PredictSon 10
11. A clouded movie 11
12. Conjure up Assurances 12
13. The might in portrayal 13
14. Angels, lured 14
15. Sea of thoughts..15
16. If I could, would I? 16
17. An Artist goes live 17
18. Quite often.. 18
19. Seaside stays 19
20. Media and its euphoria 20
21. Park thy mind 21
22. A battle against time - Tesla............................ 22
23. Aberrations in life.. 23
24. Erase the can't 24
25. What's your Age?... 25
26. Moderation, not a demon 26
27. When you get down 27
28. To keep fighting, alive...................................... 28
29. Camaraderie of vibes 29
30. Follow your heart 30
31. Was it the smiles? 31

32.	Whimsical wheel	32
33.	For better, or worse?	33
34.	Stories untold	34
35.	Toys named books	35
36.	Possibly, mystery	36
37.	Art, unforgotten	37
38.	Yesterday, Today and Tomorrow	38
39.	Co-existence	39
40.	Acts in life	40
41.	What an imagery	41
42.	A Poet on the Moon?	42
43.	Paper planes	43
44.	JPEG and BMP - A Love Story	44
45.	A concert on April First	45
46.	With such ease	46
47.	Who thought of a Vacation first?	47
48.	Spaces, not meant	48
49.	In the mirror	49
50.	Running in circles	50
51.	The worth in craziness	51
52.	Where's the problem?	52
53.	Misled intent, opportunity pleasant	53
54.	Togetherness etiquettes	54
55.	Words to me, fantastic	55
56.	Random musings	56
57.	Ways, profound	57
58.	Beep'ology	58
59.	Welcome interventions	59
60.	Would you rather be?	60
61.	Pass it over	61
62.	Be just fine	62
63.	Notions dispelled	63
64.	Rhyming tomfoolery	64
65.	Weeps that went	65
66.	A difference, worthwhile	66
67.	A Poetry Garden	67

68. Growing bamboo shoots..68
69. Be right there..69
70. Wishing Wells..70
71. A song, one day...71
72. More can join..72
73. Things will be things...73
74. Words you rarely say...74
75. Drunken bats..75
76. Oxygen...76
77. Halo in the living space..77
78. When the dust settles..78
79. Grabbed alright...79
80. Do what you Love...80
81. Cloud Gazer...81
82. Suspension of belief..82
83. The quilted wall..83
84. Messed up stop sign..84
85. Book'ified...85
86. The four-letter word..86
87. Grilling times...87
88. The power of intent..88
89. A new buddy..89
90. Warriors in the storm...90
91. No Sugar..91
92. Meaningful Disparity..92
93. Be alright with that...93
94. Believing..94
95. Acceptance..95
96. A question to muse..96
97. Ghost stories..97
98. Won't be charity..98
99. A good reason...99
100. Harder phrases...100
101. To stay there..101
102. Shove them aside..102
103. So long..103

104. Free Books..104

105. A song, lost and found...105

106. Food'y unicorns..106

107. Another abode...107

108. Perfect songs..108

109. Men of steel...109

110. The Art of falling apart 110

111. Movies and life 111

112. My calculative mind 112

113. My beloved phone'y..113

114. The rag picker..114

115. Generations apart 115

116. Hummingbird Street...116

117. Spooky drivers...117

118. Making Art..118

119. A vacation destination, unique.................................119

120. Rise up higher 120

121. Irksome vibes...121

122. It's alright 122

123. Growing divide..123

124. A worthwhile try 124

125. You can 125

126. Wait for the turn..126

127. Lovely Ms. Air...127

128. Old Spice shaving cream..128

129. At the halfway mark...129

130. Back to the front..130

131. That little note 131

132. Radio silence 132

133. Bring along your bugle...133

134. Contemplating acts..134

135. Step-truth..135

136. Ain't such a dork? 136

137. Hang tight...137

138. Not a straddler...138

139. Promising teens 139

140. What's on your platter?.................................... 140
141. Unseen parody..141
142. Labels on Calendars 142
143. Power of thoughts...................................... 143
144. Find the light.. 144
145. From the other side......................................145
146. I may never buy a VR................................... 146
147. Not counting my miles..................................147
148. Diabetics of Love.. 148
149. When mirror flew 149
150. Blind recluses..150
151. A soul's heartburn.......................................151
152. An unraveling, unique...................................152
153. Taking shortcuts...153
154. Easy to put on 154
155. Random thoughts..155
156. The power in words......................................156
157. A Happy Birthday 157
158. Society..158
159. She's alright 159
160. Sunset or her?... 160
161. At the gates...161
162. Starkness, even in good 162
163. Breezy belief...163
164. My silly world... 164
165. If I could, you could too................................165
166. Across the finish line 166
167. Burden called perceptions..............................167
168. Not choosing sides...................................... 168
169. I race, tomorrow...169
170. Haystack in my shoe.....................................170
171. Ain't bad at all...171
172. Hello of the other side 172
173. Hypocrisy meter...173
174. Be by my right...174
175. The walks back from work 175

176. I ain't no Painter 176
177. That one song? 177
178. If I were a wallet 178
179. What's your trade? 179
180. A walk on the mountains.. 180
181. Answers to find 181
182. Predator and prey 182
183. Hardwired..183
184. Weird-some beast 184
185. Mrs. Grumpy and Mr. Happy...185
186. Gallant acts 186
187. A two-way breeze.. 187
188. Life, a parody unique.. 188
189. To another planet? 189
190. Back, behind 190
191. Days of the week 191
192. Till death do us apart 192
193. A restless ramble 193
194. Fair or unfair?..194
195. Leap off your fence 195
196. Virtual Primes 196

Prose versus Poetry

What if prose and poetry had a competition,
Which would be standing tall at the end, and with gumption?
For prose has a steady voice that knows to hold,
While poetry has a way of turning plain simple prose into gold,
But then prose is known to keep a reader drawn in, for long,
While poetry is known for the meaningful seeds that get sown,
If prose can portray a cycle of emotions like a story,
Poetry can unravel a saga in a few lines flowing symmetrically,
If prose can make you flip those pages in encapsulation,
Poetry can freeze you for moments in time, in contemplation,
If prose has a way of capturing the tiniest events in detail,
Poetry can pack pocket dynamites, as thoughts to be retained,
If prose can create a new universe out of thin air,
Poetry can compare two universes square and fair,
If prose is a way to know more, to gather wisdom,
Poetry is a way to give wings to a deeper retrospection,
If prose makes you pick up a book, huddle in a corner,
Poetry can make you rekindle moments, make your heart flutter.

—*Giridhar Rajani Jaded*

1

Twenty-Four hours called life

It's 24 hours that we all have with us,
On an even keel, if you would call it thus!
It's in these 24 that life always transpires,
It's in these 24 that life always inspires,
It's in these 24 that great battles are fought,
Inside the minds, where master plans are sought,
It's in these 24 that bastions are wrought,
In castings of iron forged while fiery hot,
The plans to then be executed on another 24,
But there are human emotions also at the fore,
Virtues, ideals, righteousness, kindness on one shore,
Hatred, envy, greed, power on the other shore.
Which shore has mightier winds that lure thy soul?
This game of lure, often seen in talks of the folklore.
There's also a few who spend their 24 hours,
Doing things in their mind, to bring out their core,
Backed with actions they proudly called their own,
To put to use the 24, in the best possible way known.

—*Giridhar Hanumanthappa Jaded*

Free Books

A random walk in the streets one fine day,

Turned out to be life changing, in a way,

For a woman spurned in her heart, down so deep,

Whose insides hurt, but she could barely weep.

It was reminiscent with her morning dream,

For there was something thrown down, for her to cling,

As she walked out her house that morning,

She was still sad, yet her heart kept nonchalantly singing,

Around a corner was a battered bookstore,

Beaten by a storm, had left many a page worn and torn,

The owner stood there with a face forlorn,

Holding a *'Free Books'* placard, hiding well his frown,

The pages left now, might not bring home the bread,

Yet turn out to be a reason to ward off some dread,

A book she picked up that day, as a mere coincidence,

In a glittering end, ended up making all the difference.

—*Giridhar Rachna Jaded*

Post card on the wall

A taped-up post card on the wall,

That stood tall over the dining hall,

Was worn out yet had the ink holding on,

For 75 years, it had really been that long,

The picture on the card was picturesque,

A halo over smiling faces looked pristine,

It was an Artist's portrayal of a future,

Where mankind reveled in a thriving placenta of Mother Nature,

After seeing the spoils of war, and its deadly aftermath,

Didn't take him much to do have done the hard math,

That wars are nothing but a mad rush towards a certain wrath,

A way of laying mines, whilst singing along, in one's own tracks,

If an Artist saw us smiling today, so long back,

Whose burden are we carrying on our weary backs?

History has the lessons galore, on many olden walls,

Why then are we having to build them human walls?

—Giridhar Pavitra Jaded

4

When the tables turn

To all the men who have been raised,

Thinking it's ok for a woman to be grazed,

In ways not meant to be, and walk around unfazed,

What does it feel like? When the night ends?

Maybe an act of anger from someplace else

Gets misplaced, swallowed, burped bereft of any sense,

And then explodes in a heinous way indeed,

Maybe from an inner need to be freed?

For if it's about a chance, life is a dance,

Get your feet in or sway out of the trance,

But standing there, making a mockery of humanity,

What pride is there in misplaced profanity?

And what joy if any, in misguided violence is there?

When the tables turn, all that'll be left will be despair.

Respect not seen is respect not shown,

Respect not shown is respect not owned.

—*Giridhar Praful Jaded*

The thoughts that fade

Would I be able to see myself?

In a life not full of oneself?

Where time is of an essence,

To try and make a little difference?

Would I be able to turn myself?

Into something not off the shelf?

With what I do, having a calming presence,

In a larger scale in some form or sense?

Would I be able to change myself?

Into something worthy to dwell?

With a lesson learnt or two gently dispelled,

For what's life without a few fears quelled?

Do thoughts like these, torment you as well?

I am just one person, what could I show and tell?

Thoughts like these are hard to wade,

But after a few moments, they gently fade.

—*Giridhar Harsh Jaded*

Shiny twigs

Did someone ever make up their mind,

To bare it all, write it without any binds,

To sit down and contemplate rather hard,

On the life that lay ahead, then onward,

For what was happening didn't make sense,

Tired of acting up so long, in pretense.

Did one pen down their thoughts as carefree words,

To act as a magic wand or a fiery sword.

And having envisioned a virtual future,

Like a well laid out plan, meticulously mature,

And then followed the breadcrumbs of that master plan,

With a belief that if anyone, only I can?

An end to a story like that, isn't hard to predict,

For if our mind has tricks, life owns that gig.

In a humongous forest, we are all shiny little twigs,

Each trying to dispel in its own swiveling jig.

—*Giridhar Viaan Jaded*

Together

How many times have we seen?

In a movie, fantasy or even fiction,

That the world as is stands divided,

Until a threat to humanity has arrived,

And out of the blue everyone just unites,

Reinforcements, shelter, acts of kindness alike,

To fight a threat, together as mankind,

And a few heroes with their valor, leave us in a bind,

For in the end, in humanity standing together,

We emerge from the trauma, feeling stronger,

But do we ever stop, reflect and then ponder,

If a sequel was made that went a step yonder?

Where the world reveled in that feeling of oneness,

And hung on to it, not again to isolation and loneliness,

Or would there be another twist in the tale,

When prosperity is all places, none looking pale,

Would humanity find newer ways to then divide,

Or to move on ahead as one, leaving petty anomalies by the side?

—*Giridhar Krustappa Jaded*

8

Technology for a cause

Looking at them eyes strained from reading,
Reading pages inside a tablet, not a book or a magazine,
It's a wonderful sight to see Some reading,
In today's world where time, is forever receding.
And in that act of virtually reading,
Mother Earth starts to heal, least a beginning.
And then I think about the umpteen times at work,
That I have made notes on a notebook,
In the past though, now replaced by mental notes, keystrokes,
Paper in a trash, a sight to silently loathe,
For maybe it's time to take a stronger oath,
To not quell more trees, to recycle a lot,
Do not be a fool, read them books like crazy,
The essence of a book the same, buy used books even if creasy.
Or a $20 tablet, as a federal mandate,
To everyone in IT, to make notes all ways,
Wonder how many a tree will then live on,
Pushing the impending slowly into the oblivion?
—*Giridhar Deviramma Jaded*

Mr. PredictSon

A man fondly known as Mr. PredictSon,

Had a hefty paunch growing like a mansion,

A sham of a mustache, in a style his own,

Pointed at the ends, twisted and outgrown,

He wore brown thick rims that made him look sixty,

While he really was hobbling around to his fifty.

He carried no grimace at the way he looked,

For the cover of his book was painted by his work.

A dry bark on the ground is a possible fire,

Only with a desire, an enabler like Oxygen, and of course fire,

He had a gift, a love affair with numbers,

Sat at a desk, predicted those storms and thunders,

Once in a while he thinks about that workout,

Global warming demon though, it runs amok,

And when an enabler has their tasks cut out,

The only option is to devotedly dive or move on out.

At times he works for days around the clock,

Wondering if someone out there would turn it back for him, a notch.

—*Giridhar Kashibai Jaded*

A clouded movie

Instead of watching a movie one day,

I decided to reinvent a childhood play,

For I wasn't in the mood for the mundane way,

To sit for hours and then to stare away.

I sat out in the patio and watched the clouds,

And soon enough, initial credits rolled,

A few birds came into the view, danced away,

I was struck by awe, as my heart began to sway.

I remember that memory from long ago,

In one of those moments of life, hard to forego,

I used to let the shape of the clouds,

Unravel to me and speak out uninhibited and loud.

I wonder if it's the same clouds from childhood,

Have made it across oceans, through hot and cold,

Those shapes now became mesmerizing actors for me,

In what appeared to be nature's self-made movie,

And as I relished in a few moments and breathed,

A sigh of relief quivered, and it slowly escaped.

Soon enough the sky became rather cloudless,

The birdies did their credit roll, and I sat there in silence.

—*Giridhar Manohar Jaded*

Conjure up Assurances

As I walked besides a river one night,

When the sky was lull, no stars shining bright,

With the night's lunar glow masked by artificial light,

I happened to notice that a beaming light,

From a streetlight across the river made a wonderful sight.

It created a shimmering halo in water – a halo just right,

I stood for a moment, and felt the night dawn,

A preferred view any day, against an idiot box and a yawn,

And I walked along a few more steps long,

And I noticed the halo in water gently cascading along,

I wonder if this is real or fiction in my imaginary mind,

For my mind's adept at enlivening fantasies, like a careless wind,

And that's when I make a coerced, yet calming conclusion,

It followed me not blindly, maybe with a certain reason,

The path I tread seems to be the right direction,

I smile on knowing reassurances can even be from imaginations.

—*Giridhar Padma Jaded*

The might in portrayal

A Transsexual human somewhere, rages a battle,

To create an identity, like the two sexes with societal mettle,

And though the battle has moved on to more greener lawns,

There are always wolves lurking between them fawns,

A Transsexual who had a dream conquered, in real,

Won a gold medal lifting weights, heavy metal

But what wasn't seen in that glittering receptacle,

Was the weight carried all through, avoiding them debacles.

The weight from the world, seeing different,

In someone with just as much of an innocent existence,

Won a gold after having cleared many a tests,

Played it fair, got accolades and little pecks,

The story in the media though, is more on the wolves,

Who seem to have stolen the thunder, with their wicked howls.

A controversy is also one of the possibilities,

Why does do we let it swallow the delicacies,

The delicacies of life in Kindness and Compassion,

And a responsibility to uphold true grit, unrelenting passion.

—*Giridhar Linganagouda Jaded*

Angels, lured

The stage was lit up in glittering lights,

At least a thousand eyes had set their sights,

Onto a stage that had been chosen right,

To bring out the best nightingales out that night,

A few came along and set the stage on fire,

Not just with their voice, by moving like wild wire,

The night was ablaze, just like a magical choir,

As singers unleashed their vocal repertoire.

Between a receding applause, in walked a girl,

Simply dressed, pushing on a wheelchair, brow twirled,

Was evident she was concealing an army of nerves,

Her voice shivered even as she fumbled with words,

But on a cue, she closed her eyes, she started to sing,

Angels from skies landed, leaving behind their kings.

For what they had heard was a sacred act of singing,

That withheld a soul's pure joy in believing.

—*Giridhar Geeta Jaded*

Sea of thoughts

The waywardness of human thoughts,

Is like a spider caught up in knots,

From a wind that wreaked havoc,

Twisting and turning the web, entangling it whole,

Like a fleeting thought about a place,

Erased by the missing presence of a face,

Erased by a compelling thought, leaving behind a trace,

Replaced by a thought about a dirty shoelace,

I wonder if it was always meant to be a maze,

For an open mind to wander free, and graze,

And while on a feeding frenzy once a while,

A thought hits back home, brings along a smile,

Or a random walk into a darker place,

Brings back memories with a darker trace,

At other times, waywardness helps trod that extra mile,

And sometimes just keeping that hungry mind occupied.

—*Giridhar Vijayalakshmi Jaded*

If I could, would I?

If I could silence the voices in my head,
Would I then call myself, well off and rested?
If I could lock myself up in a corner,
Would I be safe from all kinds of danger?
If I could freeze my feelings, and kill that flutter,
Would I be cold towards all the people that matter?
If I could somehow suspend my conscience forever,
Would I run amok conquering my desires?
If I could stop trying to get any further,
Would I be like an obscure stone, one that doesn't matter?
If I could run away from poverty and hunger,
Would I reach a place where equal opportunities matter?
The if's and but's of life shall go on forever,
Getting to a better place, is it all that matters?

—*Giridhar Ashok Jaded*

An Artist goes live

An Artist empties his soul out on a stage,

At a certain avenue that's well commercialized,

The crowd loiters around, looking for a place,

To dine in and spend an hour or two any which ways.

The singer tries harder to get his voice be heard,

Pitching it to that beauty, that teen boy and that nerd,

It took a while for the peeps to be seated,

Took a few tries, and the order re-repeated.

The open air was warm, and it smelled of beer,

With music in the air, heard even far away – crystal clear.

A few stood around, listened respectfully a little while,

Admiring a nuance or two of a Singer going live.

And it wasn't that hard to not notice that faint little smile.

Some though walked around, more lost than a teenage crush,

While some hobbled on out, dreading that bumper crunch.

An evening like this is a replica of sorts,

Replayed every evening as another Artist bares it all out.

—*Giridhar Ramanagouda Jaded*

Quite often

A simple act of seeing people as people,

So simple, yet often found in a bin-recycle,

For when this competing world it beckons,

Kindness is often fed to them hungry falcons.

And in one's own innocent hunger to succeed,

Many a rule are bent, often lured by pure greed.

At what point does one look back and think,

Or contemplation seldom occurs, and life goes on in a blink?

A simple act of respecting people as people,

So simple yet seen in held back trickles, also so feeble.

Why be mean, when it's all meant to be freed,

Why kill the Bee whilst all you crave is her sweet?

The power of conscience, it's a gift given to everyone,

Wonder why it lay secluded, ever so painstakingly often?

—*Giridhar Anysuya Jaded*

Seaside stays

To make a home, an abode alongside a beautiful seashore,

Isn't that a rather resilient dream from the folklore?

For the mystique and the lure of the sea,

Is there across centuries, to be seen.

For with the sun beating down all the time,

Or at least shining bright most of the time,

With a feeling of feeling cold only inside the hearts,

While the weather smiles on feeding wanting hearts.

Like an act of being rude believing it to be bold,

Is like sifting through sand, looking for non-existent gold.

Yet maybe it's the warmth from outside that seeps deep inside,

Into the hearts of ones that gratefully reside,

For what else explains those warmhearted people,

Who smile more often, seem to hold life on a throttle?

To call seaside hotels as being vaguely commercial,

Isn't a whole truth, even though somewhat real,

To make a stay at a seaside modestly possible,

Was also a worthwhile act, and in its own way noble.

—*Giridhar Subhash Jaded*

Media and its euphoria

A fleeting like far across from Paris,

A like sailing across from Versailles,

A comment back home from India,

A share from a corner in far across Indonesia,

An affirming like from the Emirates,

A floating like from ones who say Hi as 'YAY Mate',

I wonder at the power of this phenomenon called Media,

Sharing with the world, its own hypnotic euphoria,

A sparkling like from a place in Rio, Brazil,

A like from someone reading under a windmill,

The words that once made a home deep inside,

Have found a way to be on the outside,

And it doesn't matter which backyard or seaside they ride,

For I let them out Like I had nothing to hide,

And if in a way, my words cause your heart to glide,

Into a few moments of feeling apart, its then I smile,

And I feel more alive every single time,

Someone dweller of words somewhere likes a few thoughts of mine.

—*Giridhar Myna Jaded*

Park thy mind

If there's a place in time where I can,

Place my mind a while, and adorn some tan,

Not before spraying a sea of sunscreen,

To protect what's left of my shade unseen,

For my mind I think is an ocean at best,

With creatures inside, friendly yet filled with unrest,

They call for action of the mysterious kinds,

While I try to sort the vibes in my mind.

And when at a real ocean, just looking on,

I have an inkling as to what goes on,

As soon as I park my mind, the two oceans collide

Two worlds fight, animosity by their sides,

I look around, listen to a song, and read along,

Letting the two worlds sort it out on their own.

—*Giridhar Vasundhara Jaded*

A battle against time - Tesla

When do you call something in hindsight?

As a thot or concept, ahead of its times?

Is it when its boundaries cross what already exists?

Or from those reactions that are hard to predict?

For if there wasn't a chance taken anytime,

Would we have a million answers already in line?

For someone who thinks ahead of their time,

Is watching out silently for their own kind,

Not a bunch of loved ones, but all of mankind

In a quest to onboard them believers behind,

One such battle being fought at this time,

By a man with a vision ahead of our times,

Or so we hope, but maybe it's fought just in time.

Tesla fights a battle against sands of time.

—*Giridhar Shrikant Jaded*

Aberrations in life

Aberrations also can be kin in life,
For they as well can soothe just fine,
Like the constant whirring of a worn-out fan,
Standing tall on an iron rod stand,
It's been long gone in the sands of time,
It blasted a while and rattled the remaining while,
Molten into something new by now,
But boy did it make a memorable sound.
It's been long gone, also took childhood along,
But left memories, revelations to hang on,
And a fleeting memory of that whirring fan,
Listening to which was a lullaby night long,
Even in that irksome aberration, there was a song,
Those noisy nights seemed nice, peaceful and long.
An image of a blue stumbling fan lives on,
As I wait to hear it somewhere, one more time

—*Giridhar Pavan Jaded*

Erase the can't

Something that you really want,
Can't stand alongside the word 'can't',
For a can't has a deadly vice it uses,
Onto minds that start swaying to abuses.
An abuse in the form of an excuse,
Or in the form of a much-awaited recluse,
Or at times in the guile of being amused,
Not doing what we can, a resisting brood,
For a dream then becomes 'can't dream',
Taking you to places you should've never seen,
Even if a can't resides beside your dream,
It can be slowly erased, made unseen.
If it's something that you really want,
Would you get pulled down by a measly can't?
—*Giridhar Apoorva Jaded*

What's your Age?

'*What's your age*' someone asked an old man,
'*196*' answered the man, coming out of a police van,
For the cops found no probable cause,
Dismissed his answers as old age menopause.
The reporter was amused, let out a laugh,
Back in a studio, a boss wrote off a mark,
Everyone in the crowd was bewildered, a lot,
Came closer to the van, to hear the old man's plot.
'*What year were you born*' one asked out,
The grumpy looking man, with a belly so stout,
'1916' replied aloud, the smiling old man,
Cellphones came out,103, silent smirks for a senile man,
The old man was wise, sensed the sarcasm,
Said something next, it caused a thoughtful orgasm,
'*I lived a life where I loitered along knowing,*
That some moments are worth re-living, and re-counting'
—*Giridhar Prashanth Jaded*

Moderation, not a demon

The glistening bottles of liquor on a wall,
Alluring to the eyes, at a restaurant or a bar
To the taste buds that don't mind a sip,
It's like a blue ocean ready to be dipped,
But in hindsight or as an afterthought,
Have you ever sat down and thought?
If all those bottles were on your table,
Which way would your mind flutter, tremble?
For even if an ocean lay, to be explored,
It takes a deep dive to really be floored,
So is an ocean of liquor just salty and sour,
Until there's a meaning in that drink being poured
Moderation in effect isn't a restriction,
It's a way to mix a high and rationalization.

—*Giridhar Madhura Jaded*

When you get down

What's it like to get down from a train?

Knowing someone will be there, even if it rains?

To get down and look around the crowd,

For a familiar face after light years long?

What's it like to get out of a plane?

Knowing a placard awaits on a cane,

To get down knowing it's an exploration,

Of the unfamiliar in an unknown fashion?

What's it like to get out of a boat?

Knowing very well them shores won't float?

And to be in a foreign land, feeling a little lost,

And to still create moments, to raise that toast,

Moments in life come from places apart,

Yet cling on to feelings felt deep inside the heart.

—*Giridhar Mridula Jaded*

To keep fighting, alive

What does it take to be a fighter?
To make a body as one's identifier,
And to walk into a ring knowing,
It could be the end or a new beginning,
An end to a dream lived like a frenzy in the mind,
Nothing less than a few million times,
Or to lay them tracks for a train of pain,
To accept victory with them hurting veins,
What is it like to wake up, take a limping walk?
And stand in front of a mirror and then to sulk,
For even though the body looks like hulk,
The scars on the face would be hard to flush
Yet for a passion or in a hunger to win,
A fighter does swallow pain to keep fighting, alive.

—*Giridhar Kiran Jaded*

Camaraderie of vibes

Which way will those winds sway,

Towards a victory or rather a fail,

For the way in which they graze,

Can often leave behind lives in a haze,

What they carry, is worth in gold,

Vibes that we let around, to surround,

From the thoughts and people around alike,

A lot resides on those itsy - bitsy vibes,

For them vibes can surprisingly turn the tides,

Of the rogue winds towards the right,

If egged on by the heartfelt vibes,

All else shall in time fall in place.

If anything, a camaraderie with vibes,

Is also an experience worth relishing, reliving in life.

—Giridhar Tejraj Jaded

Follow your heart

If there's a fire inside your heart,

Let it be for the things right,

If there's a belief inside your heart,

Let it be for things big and bright,

If there's a desire inside your heart,

Let it be for things without knives,

If there's a fight inside your heart,

Let it be for things worthy of a fight,

If there's a dream inside your heart,

Let there be actions, don't just let it slide,

If there's a fear inside your heart,

Let there be a stare, back into its eyes,

If there's a life inside your heart,

Leave them rustic vibes aside, follow your heart.

—*Giridhar Naveen Jaded*

Was it the smiles?

Was it love that burned them,
Or was it the hate?
Was it desire that spurned them,
Or was it the guile?
Was it the world that turned them?
Or was it the strife?
Was it hope that deserted them,
Or was it the time?
Was it care holding them together,
Or was it the unforgiving tries?
Was it a race that kept them running?
Or was it a farce?
Was it a thread binding them together?
Or was it the smiles?
—*Giridhar Nitin Jaded*

Whimsical wheel

To find a new meaning in something,

That has had a decent enough existence,

As something perceived in essence,

From seeing it as such with a lens,

A lens that has a 360 view but is screwed,

Tight around some angles, is a bit skewed,

Those angles called perceptions are the best,

In wrestling an emerging resurgence to rest,

But the eyes that shake off those lenses,

To hear a warning, yet go on to see the nuances,

Of a meaning so stark when seen this way,

I wonder why wear those lenses anyway?

To see is a gift, to un-see is a gift as well,

To see the unseen, is like riding a whimsical wheel.

—Giridhar Nandan Jaded

For better, or worse?

The things that used to move me,

Don't do so anymore,

The things that used to touch me,

Don't do so anymore,

The things that used to annoy me,

Don't do so anymore,

The things that used to torment me,

Don't do so anymore,

The things that used to hold me back,

Don't do so anymore,

The things that used to stir me,

Don't do so anymore,

The things that used to lure me,

Don't do so anymore,

The things that used to want me,

Don't do so anymore,

The things that I want to want me,

Seem to be listening, slowly working with me.

—Giridhar Deepthi Jaded

Stories untold

In times when the click of a button,

Can make once unfathomable things fathom,

Like the home delivery of fresh grocery,

Or the rarest of rare of obscurities,

Or availability of clothes with humane accuracy,

In an age where time is worshipped like currency,

And most comforts are out of creativity,

And with a healthy serving of commercial captivity,

I wonder why not a humane touch be added

To business, make them look less cold hearted,

And add a story to each order getting sent,

A story from the seller, a day in their life as it happened,

The product that was, could now be a story,

To tag along life, making own's own newer memories,

Would life stories and snippets then drive,

Businesses and would they fly low or rather high?

—*Giridhar Abhishek Jaded*

Toys named books

The best toy to hand a child is a book,

For it's a gesture of teaching them where to look,

Even if not all answers are found in books,

Reading is a process in which a brain, it cooks,

And in those early moments spent imagining,

A world that didn't exist, brought alive through reading,

The inherent hunger to learn is guided,

Into a path that's been well tried and tested.

Yet, if all the lessons were in the books written,

It would take at least a hundred good books to really awaken,

Yet books open doors, and also close a few,

Closing ones which if left open, could lead to hurdles new,

Let there be toys, let there also be books,

Help them conquer hurdles at every little nook,

Like a log of wood is priceless for a drowning person,

Books are them salient candles in a nurtured evolution.

—*Giridhar Shwetha Jaded*

Possibly, mystery

If possibility is a positive word,

I say, possibly is a mystery word,

For the manner in which it is used,

And pertinently on whom it is used,

Not to forget the context it was used,

Can evoke reactions so stark, one's often left amused.

The word possibly, used to instill hope,

On a possibility to a seven-year-old,

Or the word possibly, used to ward off a jolt,

Falsely leading one to hang onto a hope,

Profound effects from light to the dark,

Possibly can have an everlasting impact

How well do words assume responsibility?

In turning a possibly into a possibility.

—*Giridhar Avinash Jaded*

Art, unforgotten

An 80-year-old man who still walks well,
With a smile that can make any heart swell,
Deals with a few rustic parts, over abused
In a life lived well, wonderfully bemused,
He spends four hours a day locked in a barn,
Trembling hands still loves to carry on,
For an aging body also has an aging mind,
Starting to forget things, more often with time,
But a passion of his, to make wood shine,
After carving out a beauty, neat and fine,
It tingles him still deep and well enough,
Despite his memory loss, he hangs onto his craft,
Ain't that truth enough to be stark,
A mind can wander on, but a heart clings onto Art.
—*Giridhar Pratik Jaded*

Yesterday, Today and Tomorrow

If tomorrow was just a sham,

Would we as a human clan,

Have walked so far along,

And in the process, righting wrongs?

If yesterday was just a sham,

Would we as a human clan,

Have learnt so much so soon,

Even stumbled onto the moon?

If today was just a sham,

Would we as a human clan,

Have held onto what we believe,

In a humble attempt to achieve?

Yesterday, Today and Tomorrow are here to stay,

Waiting to embrace us as kids, every single day.

—*Giridhar Karthik Jaded*

Co-existence

Two armies once marched for a battle royale,
With tanks, choppers and fighter jets along,
Flags and bastions were painted in rye,
One went as far as using blood to make an Eagle's eye,
The war was to be fought over two months,
It was meant to be long, with a few twists and turns,
For words spoken till then hadn't worked,
Nor acts of assurance, that seemed forced,
People had traveled across both sides,
Trying to curb down those raging tides,
Fight and exist, not co-exist was the viral slogan,
Engraved on every single pointed glistening gun,
A twist came when food supplies were off,
A divine intervention, it arrived as tornadoes,
At first the food, then a few blankets shared,
Nerves from deathly alleys were then spared,
And in the days that followed, magic flared,
A colony got built, co-existence got portrayed.

—*Giridhar Rashmi Jaded*

Acts in life

Some get known for a calming presence,

Some get known for a positive vibrance,

Some get known for their pure flamboyance,

Some get known for their confidence,

Some get known for their perseverance,

Some get known for their appearance,

Whilst,

Some get known for their arrogance,

Some get known for their ignorance,

Some get known for their prejudice,

Some get known well as coyoteites,

Some get known for their confusions,

Some get known for their delusions,

Every act adds a little, to which half? A good question.

—*Giridhar Preethi Jaded*

What an imagery

Of all the billion clicks every day,
That capture moments of life in every way,
Of all the pictures that get clicked away,
How many are moments of being blown away?
How many are moments not given away?
How many are moments carelessly lived away?
How many are moments to just smile, say hey?
How many a thought is deeply evoked?
When moments as pictures make their way on out,
Onto a meshed-up blanket called the Internet,
Where there's often less of hope, more to fret,
If there was a way to find all the pictures,
That felt deeper than most, were meant to be captured,
And to then paste onto a virtual wall for everyone to see,
What a wonderful sight, what an imagery!
—*Giridhar Kashi Nath Jaded*

A Poet on the Moon?

An astronaut on the moon it makes sense,
For it's not so easy, going into space,
Countless hours of work behind the scenes,
Leads to a flying caravan from the dreams.
What it must have felt to land on the moon,
Having wondered all along, even drooled,
Another species known to drool at the moon,
The poets of life, even wanting to swoon,
Ever wonder what if a poet as well landed,
Onto a moon often seen in dreams united,
And left there in solitude for a day or two,
What literature would then sneak through?
For a union with an inspiration is known,
To always have an after effect profound.

—*Giridhar Kiran Jaded*

Paper planes

A random stranger on a certain train,

Traveled the same routes time and again,

He was a certainty to be seen most days,

Dressed up differently, in blatant ways,

He always sat by a seat at the door,

Loved to feel the air don't matter hot or cold

He had a peculiar habit while he sat,

Made paper planes like it was his Art,

And by the wings, it had his name and number,

As if expecting a plane to steal a thunder,

Most would laugh it off and trash the plane,

At times in front of him, like a funny game,

The ones who looked him up, dumbfound,

He'd landed on Mars, written a book on life.

—*Giridhar Kotish Jaded*

JPEG and BMP - A Love Story

A guy named Jpeg was born in the 90's,

Listened to jazz a lot, he was quite freaky,

He had a girl named Bmp who spoke very softly,

She kept to herself a lot, avoided superficiality,

They fell in Love through a display of colors,

In a portrayal of pride across with vibrant fervor,

The eyes that dispelled in colors remained the same,

But then age caught up to jpeg and bmp, so did fame,

They still perform royalty shows at random,

For those eyes still hooked to loyalty in tandem,

A new visual sensation, that has now gone viral,

Is up for the world to see, admire and to dispel,

This decade belongs to the Gif's of now,

The gifs rock and roll while jpeg and bmp still in Love, smile on.

—*Giridhar Aanshi Jaded*

A concert on April First

The curtains were drawn wide open,

As a mild melody played in the background,

It seemed like the air outgrew them sounds,

For those speakers quick-fired unrelenting rounds,

The music went on and for some moments of time,

The audience was dispelled in them rhymes,

Only to realize a little later, that an empty stage still beckons,

An Singer running late, they smirked and reckoned,

The music slowly shifted gears, and so did the lights,

Suddenly getting dark, hinting an oncoming entrance,

The anticipation grew, a few restless whistles flew,

All hands in the air, this audience just knew,

Lights went out, every right hand in the air,

Glowed in neon words '**Be Amazed**' -a magic show name.

—*Giridhar Ananya Jaded*

With such ease

Far aren't the days when houses r built,

With TV screens into the walls fitted,

And well-made pieces of houses assembled and planted,

In a few hours, for a home to be created.

Far aren't the days when the houses get sold,

With acts like a retina scan, lo and behold,

From where we were to where we came,

Hasn't all this been one head turner of a game?

A lifetime cherished dream for someone, is,

Created in a matter of hours, with such ease.

Put a human in harsh wilderness and in just two days,

Worries of this world forgotten, it comes down to ways,

To find that food, that shelter that feeling of Love,

Not much else the heart craves out there, till one's grave.

But how long does the home hang around,

For the journey to getting there, made painstakingly long,

Was that meant to be, is something wrong?

I might be hyperventilating, let me hear a song.

—*Giridhar Amit Jaded*

Who thought of a Vacation first?

Whoever conceived the idea of a vacation,

Must have been hit by a tornado of boredom,

Or must've ears hurting, for voices heard so often,

Would've haunted relentlessly in unison,

To carve out a way out of the usual,

To feel different for a bit, even unusual,

And in those moments lived, being a traveler,

Let lose what we hold, the world wanting order,

A tamed mind though held on for centuries until then,

A belief that a structured life is thy only brethren,

But one mind was more restless, and it shouted,

A few heartfelt words that then deeply resonated,

I believe that's how an idea of a Vacation was created,

Or led to naming something that already existed.

—*Giridhar Deepak Jaded*

Spaces, not meant

The farthest we think we can go,
Isn't something we are bound to,
It all hangs around what we really want to,
A truth so simple, yet very blatantly true.
For even something that's meant to happen,
Waits for them drumrolls of gumption,
From someone seeking a pure communion,
Of an idea, belief into a fruitful re-union.
The distance between where we really go,
And the places we loiter around, right now,
Is more a distance traveled inside the mind.
Aided by the body, supported in kind.
The farthest that all big thinkers went,
Were once spaces tagged as '**not meant**'.
Such is the power of pure human intent,
Its Omnipotent.

—*Giridhar Prashanth Jaded*

In the mirror

To close my eyes at a certain place,
With a sense of calm riding on my face,
Then to wake up in another place,
More calm, the expressions on my face,
Then to look around and utter a grace,
For both places seem like lucky spades.
To close my eyes in a certain state,
With a sense of belief on my face,
Then to wake up in another place,
A bolder look of belief on my face,
Then to head on them rightful trails,
Knowing well that when I look back at my face,
In the mirror, I see an eyebrow raised,
In admiration of how far I have really made,
From where I once was, that dark, treacherous place.

—*Giridhar Krishna Jaded*

Running in circles

The pure beauty of human intellect,

Has diligently and but magnificently led,

Us from the depths of utter discomforts,

From nakedness, from heat and that cold,

Into the castles of comfort, once unfathomed,

From shades with fans to heated wet suits,

From heading to work to working from home,

Comforts have come in fast and stayed along,

But some people do like to flip and turn around,

Like Businesses set up with cubes and spaces,

To simulate yet again, oh that workplace.

Work from home (WFH) wary people now pay up, go there to seek,

To share a vibe or two, alongside solutions they need,

What's inherent in us, is human interactions,

Not to forget-pure might in unified intentions,

Then why run in circles and not just tag along,

For its when shoulders rub, that walk no longer seems long.

—*Giridhar Sudha Jaded*

The worth in craziness

How do you define human craziness?

For everyone has roots, deeply transgressed,

For what's 'dude, that's crazy shit' to you,

Might in effect seem, just a sail through,

Or a trial of sorts for someone seeing big,

But playing along life, carrying on the gig.

And what's a walk in the park for you,

Might as well be an ocean, for someone to wade through,

So why label anything as crazy, just let it frenzy,

So long as it inspires, creates an opportunity.

If we saw the potent in one another's crazy,

And used it to unleash talent, then maybe, possibly,

The world will be a less insecure abode to be,

Where all march along, wiping insecurity off our Dictionaries.

—*Giridhar Shobha Jaded*

Where's the problem?

One city in the world, badly caught up in thick smog,

Decided to take things into its own tongs,

Passed a rule, using disparity in numbers,

One day odd, next day even, a game of ending numbers.

An odd-ending license plate sealed one's own fate.

Carpool at time or end up being late,

An even-ending license plate hideously filled with hate,

To keep waiting on a co-worker always late.

Vehicles on roads halved, so did fender-benders

A difference on Earth though little, it created a flutter,

Another village had a problem, though more natural,

A raging river plus needy kids yearning for a school,

Waterproof bags and brave-heart human carriers,

Joined hands, paved way for wisdom to create a flutter,

In the minds that were still learning the ways,

Alongside things that anyways get said,

What is there to solve, what's a problem?

A lot now hangs, on an answer to that question.

—*Giridhar Shilpa Jaded*

Misled intent, opportunity pleasant

Try all you can to destroy a diamond,

All it would do is to shine harder instead,

Smash it with the hardest of things or flings,

Toss it into molten lava, boy – it doesn't cringe,

For what stands between destructive intent,

And the purity in a diamond's existence,

Is a profound truth, from where it mildly hangs,

As intent alone won't lead across them grasslands

For with intent, a good reason when elopes

Boundaries are dispelled, and the air brims with hope,

To try and destroy a diamond, an act conniving,

Yet plenty attempts went for it, unforgiving,

In the end, they threw it away in anguish, in anger,

Someone tucked it in, for his would-be Lover.

—*Giridhar Kittu (Pramod) Jaded*

Togetherness etiquettes

In a place bereft of a sense of time,

Sitting in a beautiful eclectic fine dine,

With no presence other than yours and mine,

And the sound of water from the pool outside,

The lights just enough to light up your side,

Nothing but romantic melodies making time slide,

A healthy platter of delectable food blissfully served,

With a exotic choice of C_2H_5OH nice and cold,

With the weather playing Grandpa, rather nice,

In a place so often covered in sheaths of ice,

As the evening settles in, and starts to feel nice

And the pool it welcomes us with open arms,

Would my eyes stuck onto a cellphone be nice?

As moments also arrive carrying their own price.

—*Giridhar Sunil Jaded*

Words to me, fantastic

You can name me a fanatic,

You can call me a lunatic,

You can call me rather pragmatic,

You can call me hypnotic,

You can call me exotic,

But my words to me, are fantastic.

You can name me a scribbler,

You can call me a straddler,

You can call me a haggler,

You can call me a traveler,

You can call me rather dramatic,

But my words to me, fantastic.

You can name me a writer,

You can call me a fighter,

You can call me rather hypnotic,

But my words to me, fantastic.

Give me a hundred names, all over again,

I smile, as long as I have words to fill the slate,

And I feel they have that power to change a fate,

For someone seeking, someone lurking, even if late.

—*Giridhar Mamatha Jaded*

Random musings

If elusiveness is a certainty in life,

What it is, to search for a higher light?

If exclusiveness is a cloak that gets sold,

Why do some regular people shine like gold?

If possibilities are a mystery in life,

Who is to determine wrong or right?

If affinity is a natural way of life,

Why then are there walls and petty strife's?

If diversity is a recipe of a higher rank,

Why then, are there different colored tanks?

If proximity is a matter of a choice,

Why then are families scattered like them flies?

If intellect is a gift bestowed upon us humankind,

Contemplation, a birthright to which we aren't usually kind.

—*Giridhar Suresh Jaded*

Ways, profound

The roads that I see ahead of me,

Aren't roads, they are well knit mysteries,

For the haze that transcends from the skies,

Is beautiful, yet also clouds my eyesight,

The trees of mystique I see besides the road,

Don't seem to belong from this world,

For the aroma in the air it's unworldly,

A feeling of good prevails subversively.

The stones I see on the path that I walk,

They bounce a little, and sometimes talk,

For they have beautiful life quotes carved on the backs,

With a glowing ink meant to glow in the dark,

Darkness infused not from the lack of daylight,

But rather from life and its accomplices in plain sight.

I walk on not thinking about the steps I drop,

For I still see a worth in continuing in this path.

The possibilities that I see when I look around,

Quite a lot, and in inexplicable ways, profound.

—*Giridhar Shashan Jaded*

Beep'ology

Was there a peculiar probe ever made?

To tell a truth from a lie, a spade a spade,

Not through wires running through human veins,

But by pure intellect of a human brain,

For what we've achieved in technology,

Overshadows our power of adaptability,

Or has the advent of unseen possibilities,

Through the pangs of omnipresent technology,

Clouded our minds into falsely believing,

Blatant lies as also parts of life, comforting,

So comfortable that the Art or ignoring,

Is omnipresent in every part of a living.

Would there ever be a time the mind beeps,

Every time a lie is uttered or when it slips?

—*Giridhar Sunil Jaded*

Welcome interventions

When the world seems to stop a while,

In between busier moments of our life,

Brought to a stop by experiences alike,

Often when least expected, in our walks of life

Like when the first raindrops come by,

Halting the moment in an aroma filled sky,

Or when the first few flakes of white snow,

Touch upon the skin, flying high and low,

Or seeing an unknown baby smile at you,

A smile more beautiful than the skies so blue,

Those moments are worthwhile for their time,

To add a bit of imagery onto otherwise slipping time,

What's rare is also something awaited with care,

Waiting for such moments seems irksome but just fair.

—*Giridhar Sharath Jaded*

Would you rather be?

Would you rather be a glass half full?
Open to sprinkles from life, on the pull,
Or would you be a glass filled to the rim,
Blinded to possibilities, no matter slim,
Or would you act like a glass that's filled,
To keep oneself aside, life as one's guild,
Would you rather be an open book?
Open for anyone to come have a look,
Or would you rather be a poetic verse,
Free to serve on time, like a caring nurse,
Or would you rather be a book half read,
Sharing your lessons, hiding away the dread?
Would you rather be a speck on an unknown wall?
Or would you rather be a name on the map?

—*Giridhar Rakesh Jaded*

Pass it over

A boy in the summer heat stood outside,

Holding a silver envelope by his side,

Careful not to fold it and to keep it dry,

He would be making $5 if he did it right,

He was to stand there and smile at all,

Doesn't matter young, old, short or tall.

And to one passing stranger hand it over,

With nothing more said than *"pass it over"*

And run in a manner not arousing suspicion,

Yet not stick around long enough for an explanation,

The boy did it right, brought a soft toy that night,

Not knowing what was inside, he slept with a smile.

The man who opened it, read it and also smiled,

"One good deed to be done", words written inside,

The stranger did his part, wrote his deed,

And the next day another boy stood, smiling in the heat.

—*Giridhar Praveen Jaded*

Be just fine

If you can clap as well as learn, trying,
For and from the same person, you ain't wry,
You have a garden where it's ok to smile,
At good things, and to learn from trying,
If you can laugh as well as cry,
At the same thing, you ain't dry,
You have an ocean it hides inside,
Where feeling rise and fall like high tides,
To summon waves that sweep apart,
A platter of moments lived and thought,
To dispel in a moment like any other,
Yet revel in an essence unlike any other.
If you can become and un-become in time,
Guess things will turn out to be just fine.
—*Giridhar Vishal Jaded*

Notions dispelled

Someone told me once that the sands,

On the corners of the world's oceans,

Are a result of ocean life excretions,

Particularly the fish and their communion,

I was a kid and did what I did, believed,

And wondered, what did the fish feed?

Until one day in a classroom elsewhere,

My myth was busted without any care,

And after a while it made sense, even sounded fair,

That there's more to it than ears can hear,

A prank like that is alright when light,

Notions dispelled, also a way to the right,

A walk in the sands or a look at the fishes,

Makes me smiles at times, in remembrances.

—*Giridhar Ravi Jaded*

Rhyming tomfoolery

If things that are meant to be,

Do not transpire into possibilities,

Then is it right to name it reality?

For when there is an opportunity,

Needed as well, is some vanity,

Or a fearless sense of parity,

Towards creating a better reality,

And it can't be a mere necessity.

For what's a necessity currently,

Can soon turn into mere drudgery,

For something challenging sanity,

Usually hides, a larger eventuality,

That shall one, day dispel beliefs with disparity,

And draw parallels as an alternate reality.

—*Giridhar Gokul Jaded*

Weeps that went

She wept, until she could no longer weep,

She bled, until she could no longer bleed,

She slept, until she could no longer sleep,

She kept, until she could no longer keep.

But then

She smiled, like there was no pain alive,

She bloomed, like spring was the only time,

She slept, sound and fine in a new quilt,

She left, like she had nothing held.

And then

She healed like there was a lack of time,

She prospered like vintage fine wine,

She lived like the world came alive,

She reached to places no one else could thrive.

—*Giridhar Prashanth Jaded*

A difference, worthwhile

The tears that trickle down from a child's face,

There are times, when they do make sense,

Like when it's off a fall from the fence,

Or having been caught in an act of pretense,

Like from a simple realization of a mistake,

Or from wanting a new toy, or that cake,

Like from a scolding after a long wait,

Or from being grounded, give or take,

Yet there are tears of the other kind,

Not meant to ride on them little humankinds,

The tears from hunger, or from utter despair,

For no fault their own, life's just unfair,

Cast upon them by fate and our societal lair,

Where it good as long as its green, and who cares?

And yet when they find a reason enough to smile,

Their cheeks glow more radiant than glistening Nile,

If you can make a change in such children's life,

Do so now, for they as well have only one lifetime.

—*Giridhar Kiran Jaded*

A Poetry Garden

If all poems were written onto pages,
Pages waterproof and sturdy but not of plastic,
To then be cut as leaves in green,
And hung onto a tree somewhere,
And slowly build a forest of Poetry out in the open,
Would there then, be more ears willing to listen?
Would the blowing wind be any different?
Or the trees would have a silent existence?
Would some leaves flutter more than others?
Or would it be just ruffling of some feathers?
For a tree is just another tree in essence,
Until someone embraces its real presence,
Poetry as an Art-form needs a new garden,
To rekindle, remind a few things forgotten.

—*Giridhar Sandeep Jaded*

Growing bamboo shoots

The ones who feed on softened hearts,

Oh, they must have taken some darts,

Or they must love living life in parts,

For they seek solace in another's scars.

The ones who live life picking flaws,

Oh, they must be blessed with nicer claws,

Or they must love fishing in the dark,

For they seek to play in another's park.

The ones who feed on another's fear,

Oh, they must be deaf or not hearing clear,

Or they must love hiding their inner fears,

For they seek strength in another's shiver.

But with time, as such deeds pile on as heaps,

There shall be a payback for them deeds,

Like a tree forgetting to cement it's roots,

Too busy watching a persistently growing bamboo shoot.

—*Giridhar Vinayak Jaded*

Be right there

Wherever you go, no matter where,

I will find a way to be right there,

Only if you play it square and fair,

For there's no rehearsals in a Lion's lair,

But there's an act of gumption just fair,

With reactions reaching to just about anywhere,

Only if there's a vibe of good in the air,

For there's no girth in sprinkling hate into thin air,

Unless it's called for, given back fair and square,

If not, I will still find a way to be right there.

And while I am there, without getting into your hair,

I shall drop a few words from my poetic enclave,

And together in that moment of being there,

We could transcend horizons, to just about everywhere.

—*Giridhar Ramakrishna Jaded*

Wishing Wells

If all the nickels and dimes were picked,

Out from all of worlds wishing wells,

And melted as one under unforgiving heat,

Then carved into a monument nice and neat,

Would it still hang onto the Wishlist?

Of dreams so wanted, and unfulfilled,

Would there be a process then set in motion?

Of likely wishes finding a communion,

And of prayers together forming a cloud,

That would shower blessings with a thunder loud,

The wishes and prayers in nickels and dimes,

And the metal both creations of this time,

Wrought into a monument to stand the tests of time,

For wanting souls gathering with wishes, in line.

Would more of the tossed coins then make a rattle,

In the lives of people, when life's mostly a battle?

—*Giridhar Daniel Jaded*

A song, one day

I shall write a little song one day,

That shall take all the blues away,

Even if for a moment, or for a while,

To go on, one more moment in life,

The song won't have rainbows in the sky,

Nor birds having just learned to fly,

It won't have the melody of playful words,

Nor the parodies of a fast-paced world,

There won't be a picturesque mountain,

Nor a pristine lake with a central fountain,

There won't be beauty yet there will be beauty

There won't be lines or chains of hierarchies,

If anything, there will be a few words laid,

Out on a platter for the mind to be frayed.

—*Giridhar Vikas Jaded*

71

More can join

The milk that I pour into my tea,

I wonder if it has crossed a sea,

And has flown in thunderstorms to get here,

Or driven across from a forgotten farm, somewhere near,

A frail-some thought it comes on over,

I try not to ponder, but I sense a shiver,

Are we taking too much here, from nature?

Or from those little ones, milk as their fodder,

I see a post on animal abuse online,

70k likes, had 100+ comments alright,

And then a video of tiny little piglets,

Getting fed by mom, in a cute tussle, and no outlets,

This one had 4M likes, earned some green as bitcoins,

Good things shine and that's alright, but more can join.

—*Giridhar Swaminath Jaded*

Things will be things

The first time that I saw a hologram,

It was long before there was Instagram,

I was fascinated, out of my mind,

For glitter encapsulated then too, like something divine,

A little twist, a turn of the hologram,

And the colors exploded like WHAAM,

A further twist and them colors were gone,

Leaving behind a pale grey, a look forlorn,

Fooling around with a hologram then,

I found out that there's more meaning,

In everything than it seems, intriguing,

Only if the eyes dive in with a twist.

Not many holograms now flash around,

But things will be things, till the world goes round.

—*Giridhar Vineet Jaded*

Words you rarely say

The words that you nonchalantly shared,

Were the ones that in the end, bled,

And crept into spaces not intended,

Leaving behind a trail of trends,

And what did you get back instead,

An ocean full of lull, printed on glossy papyrus in black,

And in a sea of black, you stand in your tracks,

Like it's all cool, it's all alright,

But did you have a fair hindsight,

Your silence shall later on could cause some strife,

To the millions looking to unravel life,

By not sharing more of what's right.

Or by sharing more of what's, not right?

An eye to the world, can't afford to be riled,

An eye to the world, that's the Media,

Every story shared, an omnipotent idea.

—*Giridhar Amruth Jaded*

Drunken bats

It was a full moon night, yet an alley-dark,

Was bereft of any signs of life, and stood apart,

Wasn't much going on anyways, it was midnight,

Just the lurking Cats and flying Bats were in sight.

There wasn't anyone to miss some light,

But not everyone had called it a night,

Someone was awake but far out of sight,

Yet had a 4K view of this alley just right,

The Cats roamed unaware of being watched,

The bored Bats acted drunk, and flew into rocks,

The watchful eyes from a farther place,

Were amused by the Bats for they knew his race,

As one like them, thriving in the dark, to watch the night,

As the rest of the world slept cozy and tight,

The bats shook off a self-induced hangover, flew just right,

The watch-guard switched off his 4K, went on about his night.

—*Giridhar Vinit Jaded*

Oxygen

A dream I had one summer night,
Was light-hearted but worth a fright,
For it had me penniless, with a pen,
And a leather notebook named Oxygen,
I hobbled around for a wallet, found none,
I looked around for a phone, found none,
The place I stood at was under a red light,
I looked at me again, I was dressed alright.
Directions not my forte, I was utterly lost,
How do I get back home, worth a thought?
I opened the book to see the words *"Here you go"*,
And I sat down and wrote a few poems to go,
Tore down the pages and sold a paltry few,
Was enough to me all the way home though.

—*Giridhar Prabhu Jaded*

Halo in the living space

Heading out in the morning, was not an option,

It was rather a transient evolution,

An act filled with certain frigid conviction,

To venture out every day, with a certain reason,

As more reasons were found, livelihoods got defined,

The boundaries got drawn, a following in line,

Imagination is a beast, not willing to be tamed,

Technology, life, business add fun to that little game,

Comfort a demon, best kept a few feet away,

Too close and it will clip those dream-waxed wings away,

One reason of today, driven more the commercial way,

Is to create an electric halo in our own living space,

A halo that emanates from the wallet, as a violet light,

And encapsulates us in comforts from morning till night.

—*Giridhar Shivayogi Jaded*

When the dust settles

What happens when the dust settles?
After a still from life's constant jiggles,
When life is over, in a silent ensemble,
Would we still feel, emote or tremble?
What happens when the breathing stops?
Not to the flesh and the mass, but deep inside,
Where a sea of life's experiences resides?
Where does all that go in the sands of time?
Wouldn't make sense if it ended like a mystery mime,
Something to leave behind sounds about right,
For there's a surety of not carrying forward,
Things from a blissful life or a life wayward,
I am carving a path with the words I leave behind,
Hoping the human kind would one day, be more kind.

—*Giridhar Ghanshyam Jaded*

Grabbed alright

How many times do we turn on a car?

To drive somewhere nice, a little far,

And how many of those drives do survive,

The torrential rains in mind's hard drive, with replays - live?

How many times do we turn on a burner?

To eke out a dish, a real soul turner,

And how many times does it come out that way?

For there would be times, to discard it as a waste.

How many times do we walk in the sun?

To make what's left of open air, to walk or to run,

And how many of those walks are a chain,

Despite a routine, juggling priorities or through pain?

A count of such things is a number game,

That needs to be practiced and often played,

For in dispelling a layer deeper in things that feel right,

Does life come alive through moments grabbed, grabbed alight.

—*Giridhar Shrinivas Jaded*

Do what you Love

A constant existence of moments lost,
Doesn't make for an enticing plot,
For it's filled with drudgery, quite a lot,
From giving up moments on the trot,
The resistance inside to keep aside,
Moments of life worth feeling alive,
Can become a dreaded habit in time,
It can devour a healthy soul alive.
Days seem long or short, time just flies,
Before we even notice a star in the skies
Like all habits, this as well can be curbed,
'Do what you Love' those are the words.
And even if drudgery does come along,
You will've some memories to cling on.

—*Giridhar Shrinivas Jaded*

Cloud Gazer

There's a certain calm I feel at times,

When my mind is not really on the drive,

It's when I snatch a moment or two from life,

I am allowed to, at times, we talked it out alright,

These are moments I gaze into the skies,

Painted blue with them white clouds that glide,

Like a cotton ball, a green field, and kids behind,

And I feel lost, somewhere in my mind.

Not much of a star gazer, I am a day dreamer,

I find myself transform into a cloud gazer,

In puff of clouds seemingly playing catch,

I find something worthwhile to watch.

And on days that the skies are clear,

I dive into my mind, somewhere in the rear.

—*Giridhar Sumit Jaded*

Suspension of belief

Suspension of disbelief, is well known indeed
Suspension of belief, not often peeved,
An abandonment of disbelief a gift unique,
To revel in a fantasy or a mystery, unique.
But belief is on something we really know,
Having facts and notions in the back row,
Yet when watching a movie-we already know,
We cajole our beliefs and just let them go,
To unlearn a lesson, or relive those moments,
Of a journey filled with meaningful events,
If it can be suspended for a movie we watch,
Can it be suspended in real life, in parts?
To picture oneself as playing some part,
In real life, in flesh and blood, to walk life like an Art.

—*Giridhar Sambit Jaded*

The quilted wall

On a certain street in New Orleans,
Is a beat up house, by the oceans,
Holding onto not more than traditions,
Walking tall against the commercial marksmen,
For a family lives on, which still believes,
Heritage cometh first, and then the society,
Holding on to lessons and them beliefs alike,
Like it was the only known way known of life,
A walk into the kitchen with a broken sink,
An entire wall made of sewn up quilt,
That quilt on the wall, a part of their heritage,
Like a family rulebook irrespective of age,
Every time a rule was broken by one,
A patch had to be sewn onto the wall,
Abstract looking at first, now there's an emerging face,
On the quilt, a vision filled with grace,
Occasionally, on a full moon day,
The family sleeps on it, to dream them mistakes, away.

—*Giridhar Venugopal Jaded*

Messed up stop sign

That bent-up STOP sign from a wild storm,

Caused quite a few scares, like a norm,

Screeching of tires, the hissing of brakes,

A few eerie moments, filled with scares,

A Good Samaritan saw it all transpire,

Suddenly decided to give in to the desire,

Of wanting to go set things right, in time,

Before there's a crash, worse-a loss of life,

As he struggled with the rustic pole,

He was spotted by neighborhood patrol,

Picked for property damage, now waits a turn,

To have his say, the damage though has been done.

A pair of walking legs, is now hurtful arms on a wheelchair,

At times, the timing of things, not so fair.

Was perception doing the rounds that night, in the air?

—*Giridhar Shivanand Jaded*

Book'ified

If one has the time to spend an entire life,

Doing nothing, reading books all the time,

What would happen to that human mind,

Would it glow in a halo that shines bright?

Or would it shudder under wisdom's might?

Unable to welcome so much sense inside?

Or become a revolution, one of a kind,

For the answers to many a question, reside,

Nowhere else, but in the libraries that hide,

Hide in plain sight, also over the internet alike,

Hidden not by choice, being pushed aside,

By the lure, glitter of commercial mankind,

When was the last time you came close to being Book'ified?

If nothing, would you just visit one such Library that hides?

—*Giridhar Santosh Jaded*

The four-letter word

I first heard it, like heard it when I was two,

Didn't know then it had four letters, I was two,

Didn't know what it meant but now I know,

It can melt a heart or land that crashing blow.

I have seen it's red faced angry avatar,

And seen it encapsulate the nimble hearts.

It's probably the most abused four-letter word,

Used as an outcome, it's often an abusive sword

It's used in silence, it's used in pretense,

It's used for essence, it's used in presence,

It raises an eyebrow when it's not in line,

It can mend broken bridges, in due time,

I have seen myself taking many a meaningful path,

Merely from the use of four-letter Art 'TALK'.

—*Giridhar Ruel Jaded*

Grilling times

The glistening grill in the patio tells a tale,
The dew on the green grass it tells a tale,
The grass had been brown for so long,
While the grill collected dust, had a face forlorn,
But who can stop the Sun from beating down?
For summer sings along the ones who sing along,
It's taken a while to see spring come and go,
It felt like yesterday yet feels a long time ago.
The tides can't turn, but awaken I can,
To what's left of the summer, to rise and shine,
Fear of fire hasn't been in my dictionary,
Yet grilling never figured in our Pictionary.
I'm glad to have cleaned up a little mess,
Who cares, I grill like a chump or with finesse.

—*Giridhar Karthik Jaded*

The power of intent

Most often than not in the walks of life,
Stories erupt from magical events alike,
Of ones rising from ashes, as a start,
To then land on a higher pedestal, shining bright.
Or of ones wading them waters of obscurity,
Then climbing onto apostles of popularity,
Or of silent warriors who only come to light,
After having long gone, leaving behind a smile?
Of all such stories, how many do u think,
Were molded by nothing more than belief?
Ashes to stars or a way out through the scars,
Guess there's a method to madness of the stars,
As I read an article about yet another talent,
I see myself smiling, at the power of intent.

—*Giridhar Pramod Jaded*

A new buddy

The blinking cursor insistently blinks,

It's glares more prevalent, to the ones who ink,

For it has a hidden agenda to try and hide,

Beauty and depth in what's about to be typed.

But whoever said writing wasn't a fight,

Was gifted, in non-sensical ways alright,

I wonder what role does this cursor play,

When all writers want to do is convey,

A few learnings here, a few feelings there,

A few self-debated questions, isn't it just fair?

As I think, it starts to blink at me yet again,

As if I am a captive, my writing-it's game,

An acknowledging nod now starts off the wordplay,

I've made a new buddy, nun else to say.

—*Giridhar Shyam Jaded*

Warriors in the storm

What it must be like, to brave the weather,

To hang in there even when bodies shudder?

And stay wide awake, in long, howling nights,

Out in the cold or barely tucked inside,

For a winter storm, could be a final horn,

Before the eyes could see the next dawn,

And doing it knowing their life's at stake,

Without blinking an eye, like a give or take,

Soldiers out there or workmen staying in,

Those unseen corners need an unraveling,

For a sense of being is in not just being,

But in seeing, reflecting and respecting,

In finding a meaning to what's apparent,

But means so much more if seen, with rightful intent.

—*Giridhar Bapugowda Jaded*

No Sugar

She said 'no sugar' in the tea I made,
I knew it was true, that's how it was made,
I tried to pour an ounce of my sweetness,
Meh, it didn't work, she owns that business,
My hands tremble as I drop in a spoon,
As I could be bringing upon our own doom
I once had a sweet tooth, a big one at that
Fooled around, let many a teeth rot,
And I once saw, a choice had to be made,
By someone I knew, between his left and right leg,
And that kinda filled me with a chilling dread,
Couldn't imagine dying of diabetes, truth be said,
I cut down on my sweets, I just try and be sweet,
Win or lose, at least I get to hang on to my feet.

—*Giridhar Vijay Jaded*

Meaningful Disparity

On a lovely lush green elite golf course,

A child in a plead takes his first shot,

Sipping on a popsicle in the summer heat,

Affirmative his Dad admired his new feat.

Elsewhere on a barren patch in a dust filled home,

A child wearing nakedness, takes his first bite,

Having waited all day, till well before midnight,

Affirmative, Dad will be quicker on tomorrow nights bite.

On a sandalwood desk somewhere else,

A Dad drops a call with his teenage son,

And signs on two checks, one for his son,

A promise to keep, a used Ford Mustang,

The other check to an account unknown,

But with a might, that's needing an exposure, to be shown.

—*Giridhar Adarsh Jaded*

Be alright with that

If I could be that calming candlelight,
That burns itself and still shines bright,
Doesn't matter even if in a Chernobyl plant,
So long as it serves a need or a want,
I think I would be just alright with that,
For making a difference, something close to my heart.
If I could be that affirmative faint nudge,
Needed in moments caught up in a smudge,
I'd be happy to keep making that push,
Until you have found your way around your bush,
If I could be a fleeting moment in your life,
One of relief or a moment feeling more alive,
I think I would be just alright with that,
So long as your stars keep shining bright.

—*Giridhar Rajani Jaded*

Believing

It's an altogether different battlefield,

Where the true champions in life get made,

From unknown alleys to well-known academies,

Miraculous feats flourish in niche factories.

Where chimneys they spew burnt out ideas,

Mixed with ash from failures, to be burnt by stars.

A flash of brilliance is often a venture,

Out into the realms brighter or darker,

Doesn't matter which but certainly deeper,

In countless hours spent on doing things that matter,

Sweat and pain or burning eyes behind shades,

Many a mind battles quenched, shoved into everglades,

In clinging onto a belief, gripping tighter than most,

The champions of life emerge, from amidst them shadows.

Between believing and leaving, to believing and living,

There's a lot that goes into a champion's making.

—*Giridhar Hanumanthappa Jaded*

Acceptance

To be someplace else, isn't it a fleeting wish?

Comes and goes deftly like that first kiss,

To not be this way, and be somebody else,

Comes and goes too, even if rarely, be honest,

But to be oneself and to be feeling alright,

Is also a resounding victory in plain hindsight,

For what I am, is a truth only I can concur,

Believe in myself and maybe whimsical things shall occur?

For in a simple act of acceptance, it hides,

A realm where possibilities, they jump and glide,

And on one of those random, hopeful rides,

You shall see a tree, drool at it, and be dreamy eyed,

Not to forget seeing them flares from your fallacies,

Douse them one by one, bake some delicacies,

Being oneself long enough, will let you hang on,

Acceptance of oneself, is a launchpad for life to really hop off.

—*Giridhar Rachna Jaded*

A question to muse

The rattling of a keyboard is a magic,

That's magnificent and in a way hypnotic,

For what it can achieve in its essence,

Surpasses non-existent realms and transgresses dreams,

The million lines of information shared all over,

The lines of code holding technology together,

The forms of Art created from the world all over,

The lines typed up, erased or kept under cover,

The words shall flow, no matter what the form,

For some breathe words, or need words to feel the norm,

A keyboard, it carries on the pen's legacy,

As Evolution beckons yet again, with a contingency,

Touchscreen revolution indeed, could be the new pen,

Or dictating onto a device from speech recognition,

The forms shall change like them favorite tunes,

Is Art still making a difference, a question to muse?

—*Giridhar Pavitra Jaded*

Ghost stories

What would it be like to be that ghost,
Be that uninvited presence, with an unaware host,
And be able to hear, listen, also feel lost,
In stories being told, from a wrinkled past,
In a shelter for the elderly, faintly hanging on,
To a life nearing an end, as the body wears on,
Reminiscing memories of the good and the bad,
At times joyful, other times a story, painstakingly sad,
For when such rare stories do get told,
There's unraveling of worlds lo and behold,
For life can twist and turn in a million mysterious ways,
Every twist a story, every turn another day,
Would a story told, have a soulful meaning?
That would drive a ghost to come out of its hiding.

—*Giridhar Praful Jaded*

Won't be charity

The books that shall flow out of me,

If they end up making any money,

That's if there are eyes that still see beauty,

Hidden deftly in an Art called Poetry,

Where thoughts are never in a symmetry,

Yet gel into one another through creativity,

And flow out as lines, flirting with mystery,

Other times provoking thoughts aplenty,

If my words end up stacking up some green,

It's too early, but from what I've seen,

There's a lot to do, it won't be charity,

But rather an investment in opportunity,

I pledge 11% of all that green all along,

To make a difference in more ways than one.

For if there's a Satanic hunger in just receiving,

There's a Godly essence in the act of Giving.

—*Giridhar Harsh Jaded*

A good reason

I wonder how or why a pen was invented,

Was it for a need to keep a tab on deeds,

Or a soulful need of Art running free,

I wonder how or why a phone was invented

Was it to build a bridge in the human race,

Or a yearning heart's need to wanna connect,

I wonder how or why a TV was made,

Was it to fill some voids with images instead?

Or for a larger message to be spread,

I wonder how or why a mirror was invented,

Was it to find beauty in oneself unlike,

Or with an intent to find what's inside,

Reasons aplenty, but as an afterthought,

One good reason suffices needs, often a lot.

Or a random act of something new being found out,

Turns a good reason enough to touch a few lives, maybe a lot.

—*Giridhar Viaan Jaded*

Harder phrases

I will wait for you, is a harder phrase,

I will pray for you, more filled with grace,

For you know you can wait only when you reach,

If the road never ends, where is it that we seek to reach?

I will change for you, is a harder phrase,

I will work with you, more filled with grace,

For change is from being driven, not coerced along,

The walks of life, often reveling and seemingly long.

I will die for you, is a harder phrase,

I will live for you, more filled with grace,

For the senses no longer respond then on,

The option death would leave, just moving on.

I will be there for you, is the best phrase indeed,

Doesn't say a lot but says a lot indeed.

—*Giridhar Krustappa Jaded*

To stay there

The air blowing through your hair,

Doesn't it wear a look of despair,

For all it wants is to stay there,

In the darkness of your lovely hair.

The water rushing beneath your feet,

Doesn't it claw at the sand beneath,

For it wants to feel your silken touch,

Even as the fishes fight for a smooch,

The sound emanating from your lips,

Doesn't it move, mesmerize like hips,

For all it does is linger in the thin air,

Like music to ears, it all seems so fair.

If I could, I would be the wind, the water and that sound,

That could keep waiting for you to be around.

—*Giridhar Deviramma Jaded*

Shove them aside

That place in your heart filled with hate,

Is exactly where I have a decorated plate,

With a lavish serving of hope and positivity,

That seems like my bench-mates till eternity,

For I wasn't carved out of poverty,

Neither from being besotted with disparity,

I guess I was carved out of mere vanity,

Vanity from realizations of life-aplenty,

Those eyes of yours filled with guile,

Also quiver a little from what they hide,

In realms I foray into, I shove them aside,

For there ain't no dummies halting my slide,

If anything, I will fill that empty hate with pride,

Only if you dispel notions and walk side by side.

—*Giridhar Kashibai Jaded*

So long

I am letting myself float away into space,

At times dispelling into thin air, without a trace,

What I find there is a thread, flickering many ways,

I shall hang on, with a bold look on my face,

I am letting myself drift into those corners,

Forever evaded and kept under the covers,

For in these moments of just letting go,

Is a peace unknown, addictive, to then let go,

Without a clue as to what awaits on the other side,

I dive in, with my arms stretched out, far and wide,

What I shall find, I know would be my own,

Might be a whimsical unraveling, till then unknown,

I like to walk on for it's been really long,

Since I dispelled into the unknown, so long.

—*Giridhar Manohar Jaded*

Free Books

A random walk in the streets one fine day,

Turned out to be life changing, in a way,

For a woman spurned in her heart, down so deep,

Whose insides hurt, but she could barely weep.

It was reminiscent with her morning dream,

For there was something thrown down, for her to cling,

As she walked out her house that morning,

She was still sad, yet her heart kept nonchalantly singing,

Around a corner was a battered bookstore,

Beaten by a storm, had left many a page worn and torn,

The owner stood there with a face forlorn,

Holding a *'Free Books'* placard, hiding well his frown,

The pages left now, might not bring home the bread,

Yet turn out to be a reason to ward off some dread,

A book she picked up that day, as a mere coincidence,

In a glittering end, ended up making all the difference.

—*Giridhar Padma Jaded*

A song, lost and found

A song long lost in the memory train,
Thousands of trailers left behind,
Pops out into existence as if summoned,
From the dead, to give me an affirming nod,
By unraveling a memory, of a point in time,
When a loved one so dear, was still alive,
The song though isn't connected in any way,
But has something that makes me sway,
For it brought me a fleeting little memory,
Of when I listened to it amidst tomfoolery,
That moment in time felt magical for a bit,
And the lost and found song made a silent exit,
As one of my favorite songs made an entry,
Bringing me back to realistic reality.

—*Giridhar Linganagouda Jaded*

Food'y unicorns

A squeaking squirrel it woke her up,
As the morning haze began to eke out,
She looked around still in half a dream,
Loosely holding on to the unicorn-ice cream,
A restraining order, self-reinforced,
Meant a love affair with sweets-ignored,
A smile popped on her face, with another squeak,
As the squirrel perched onto that peak,
The yellow skies they looked picture perfect,
Like an amalgamation of colors deft, yet faint,
She brewed a coffee and tossed out a toffee,
Another unicorn of hers, kept merely for charity,
Strange how things forbidden for oneself,
Could still end up making a little difference.

—*Giridhar Geeta Jaded*

Another abode

Those paths in life, ones that we seldom tread,

Are probably factories dispelling fear and dread,

With chimneys spewing black smoke out,

And with haunting, slanted ferns on the road,

The ferns they bend over in an attempt,

To transport hate, anger and utter dissent,

From roots where negativity, it brews constant,

Swaying in wily winds, thunder persistent,

The wind in a playful mood, it toys around,

With the black smoke, often tossing it around,

Burning eyes, a pumping heart, a blurry path,

A road, seeming none less than a shot in the dark,

If everyone wandered into their fearful roads,

Would we all meet elsewhere another heavenly abode?

—*Giridhar Vijayalakshmi Jaded*

Perfect songs

Where do those perfect songs hide?

Sometimes when I am wanting a nice little ride,

For all I want to do then, is to glide,

To jump, feel, drop on a careless slide,

I hobble around not finding the track,

Until a low blow awakens me with a smack,

As I have a few deeper songs in my shack,

With some of them, that land a thwack,

And I feel calmer knowing I'll be back,

Carrying few soulful songs on my back.

And before I know I am already lost,

At times in words, other times a trance,

Even when the same songs feel apart a lot,

I hold on to them, for they do mean a lot.

—*Giridhar Ashok Jaded*

Men of steel

Some men they wander into deeper realms,

With a halo around, a protective screen,

For what they set out in life to achieve,

It relies a lot on impossibilities, in which they believe,

I wonder from where they summon that halo,

Keeping immune from life's constant innuendos,

For when they set out going on about their job,

There's not much time to shiver or sob,

A look in their eyes and you see it there,

A steely resolve and a beckoning glare,

In the end, they leave behind a legacy,

None less than a hopeful hypnotic fantasy,

A crazy like none other, drives them to do things,

That seem insurmountable at first, then mere things,

For it's in How they nailed the confusions inside,

Do most answers to grandiose and pride, reside.

—*Giridhar Ramanagouda Jaded*

The Art of falling apart

In all the times that we humans have evolved
How many a notion have been dissolved?
Strange too are the ways we have evolved,
Stranger are the boundaries that we've crossed,
From dreaming to fly one day, to flying for dreams,
From living to survive, to transcending new realms,
One such evolution is the Art of falling apart,
When dispelled into situations not driven by choice,
For it's in such moments of breaking apart,
Into pieces not easy, to be gathered and joined back,
And then to keep struggling, to make them match,
Into shapes only our imagination can seldom catch,
Natural calamities and disasters akin to that scary movie,
Putting a squabble or anger to rest, for thwarting fear assumes a priority,
In falling apart, there is an opportunity slimy, it hides,
And in joining back for better, there lies evolution inside.

—*Giridhar Anysuya Jaded*

Movies and life

The movies we watch are well chosen,

Err I take that back, let's say more often,

Having heard a word, or seen a trailer,

Having read a review, or from a workplace chatter,

Which one of those stick around longer?

A deeply moving movie, with not much banter,

Or an inspiring movie of hope, that does matter,

Or a movie of Love redefining the very word,

Or a joyride of a movie, more a laugh riot,

Or a movie about when life hits a jackpot,

Or a movie provoking thought, deep inside,

Where answers to the harder questions reside?

At times the answers we seek are in a movie,

For Art can be an eye opener, or a way to something merry.

—*Giridhar Subhash Jaded*

My calculative mind

Of all the things I could do for you,

Tell me what you like seeing me do?

For then I shall dive in, into my own,

To run a validation algorithm my own,

Where I shall see the act in all its glory,

Run a virus scan for adverse anomalies,

And weigh it on a scale for an impact,

Red for positive, green for negative as a popup flash,

Then do an anti-algorithm again my own,

To find what I could do without having known,

What you like me doing, find an act my own,

And if I see a flash of green, steady and strong,

I would do what I do best, and walk along,

Or surprise you in bettering your ask -So long.

—*Giridhar Myna Jaded*

My beloved phone'y

I have had my love-hate affair with a phone,

At times short and sweet, other times engaging and long,

I have had those fearsome thoughts as well,

About living a life without a phone - oh well,

A momentary ding or a flash is all it takes,

For my hands to lift her with a bated breath,

To dispel in her depths like a sailor - lost,

Soon realizing it's a maze meant to be lost.

Had an incident somewhere high, that opened up a door,

To live a day or two without a phone - O dear,

I did have my moments driven by that fear,

But there was also a calm presence, fleetingly near.

Strange how an incident can carve a lesson away,

To teach us something we should have learnt anyways.

As I type up another poem on my phone,

I feel stronger dealing with that Phone'y anxiety - well known.

—*Giridhar Vasundhara Jaded*

The rag picker

The bracelet he wore on his right hand,

Was something he earned, not given to him in kind,

Earned through toiling hard often times,

Or from wading through them mazes in his mind,

What he had done was now a feat well known,

With seeds of his deeds ages ago, sown,

He had started small, then built a cauldron,

Built with bricks from talents, ones chosen,

Like the time he picked up a rag-picker,

Got him a job as a sorting unit supervisor,

Or the time he picked up a homeless man,

Got him a job as a Braveheart weatherman,

Or the time he picked up a Graduate dishwasher,

Gave him a job as a playschool English tutor,

His bracelet read 'The Rag Picker,

He found something mistreated as rag, turned it to something better.

—*Giridhar Shrikant Jaded*

Generations apart

The warmth in the heart of a person,
Was once good enough of a reason,
To know them better, for a communion,
Of seeing, believing, and learning in unison.
The money in the hands of a person,
It cast a spell, held hordes of people in abduction,
To earn more or be with someone rich, not poor,
In misunderstanding life as grim, if not rich, just poor.
The information gathered about a person,
Is now a lucid goldmine valued in zillion's?
Scrounging in open, and in private for information,
Know them well to nail them well – the new revolution.
Wonder if we will ever see a generation,
'What helps thrive inside?' As a pertinent question.
—*Giridhar Pavan Jaded*

Hummingbird Street

A random jaywalk in the green woods,

With a 20% charged earphone for the mood,

I walked along that morning, knowing very well,

That directions aren't my forte, truth to tell,

But something told me to walk along,

Had a belief that I will come back nice and sound,

A curvy turn here, a wider turn there,

With not much, a lot of green everywhere,

The empty patios, the beautifully kept patios,

The hangings of heritage, the one-off scarecrows,

Those trees with mysterious shapes,

Those trickles of water from the unseen caves,

The songs kept changing, as I kept walking,

And after a while, the roads started talking,

Made friends with me, the street signs smiled,

I'll remember *Hummingbird street* alright,

As a fleeting memory, and an enlivened hindsight,

That jaywalking is one of nature's delights.

—*Giridhar Apoorva Jaded*

Spooky drivers

Some people they breeze through the roads,

Often pissing off the ones they cross,

What if it was them running against clocks?

That are not timed like ours, rather set as rocks,

For the comforts of our own routine,

Can be a big moment for someone, avoiding a late entry-penalty,

Or for that matter (and God forbid) life threatening,

For someone driving by, like a crazy being.

Yet at times, it's so hard to not go ahead and chime,

That button for it can feel liberating at times,

Not with intent, but driven by candid times,

And after having honked comes a hindsight,

Of someone probably in need, getting yanked at,

But then again what if it was just another idiot,

A smile come on, thinking maybe I was right.

—*Giridhar Prashanth Jaded*

Making Art

It takes a lot to pick up a form of Art,

For it's a proclamation of standing apart,

In trying to define a new way at something,

Which is worth wondering about, and enticing,

And standing apart does come with glares,

And those amused contemplating stares,

For wat makes so much sense to an Artist,

Might seem a mere amusement for an anarchist,

But being dispelled in a world one's own,

An Artist lives to leave a trail, a tale well told,

Often wondering how far the Art shall reach,

Often believing that their Art could, heal,

If nothing, leave behind some feelings deeply felt,

Or a few hearts that made sense of their Art, rather well.

—*Giridhar Madhura Jaded*

A vacation destination, unique

On a certain mountaintop under the sun,
There's a dictionary without the word inhibition,
And a library with only books of positivity,
With half the aisles raving on about creativity,
The air in there, oh it infuses a mystery,
The presence in there, induces tomfoolery,
For the mind basking under a shining sun,
Fooling around creating beauty one's own,
It shall be lured into few moments of joy,
Stepping onto the mountain wanting to try,
For everyone's an Artist in some little way,
On that mountain, you can spin, and let it play,
Where a visit is to a creative temple inside,
Traveled and lived more outside, but felt more inside,
Is there a place like that for a vacation?
Where creativity is a way of being, not a destination?
—*Giridhar Mridula Jaded*

Rise up higher

Does brilliance lose its shine?

Slowly under the sands of time,

Or still find its way to it's prime,

From pages of those historical vines,

For what's beautiful one day,

Will always be beautiful in a way,

Visible only to the eyes that seek,

Into perennial existence, and take a peek,

Into the past and the present alike,

As to how brilliance once, shone bright,

Soon enough, for those seeking eyes,

There shall be a glimmering light,

To hold on to as a vision, then to turn right,

Onto walks that should have been taken long ago, in hindsight.

A teeny spark or a burning fire,

To turn the tables, and to rise up higher.

—*Giridhar Kiran Jaded*

Irksome vibes

I often see you around, quite a lot,

At times noticing, other times not,

You come like the rain, leave like the wind,

Often in a few moments, but leaving in kind,

And it's not really done, what you leave behind,

Inklings of those inflicting doubts in my mind,

Having seen you, seen you well for a while,

I now know what's behind your wily guile,

For before even I step into that realm,

Where you start to try and snatch away my dreams,

I have my plans made, I anticipate you,

Knowing well, I am gonna see you through,

I see you but I un-see you as well,

No place for irksome vibes in places I dwell.

—*Giridhar Tejraj Jaded*

It's alright

A four-year-old when learning to ride a bike,
Is filled with fear at the first fall alright,
But when a word of assurance is behind,
Fear turns into an adventure, one of a kind.
In that little moment of lending a hand,
A child learns the meaning of '*it's alright*',
A few days later when the falls are less,
Fears having subsided, almost put to rest,
An adventurous turn leads to a bigger fall,
This time not turning around, hearing a silent '*it's alright*',
And in that moment of not looking back,
And being left to fend and get back on up,
Is a lesson learnt that there is a light?
In getting back up and saying, '*It's alright*'.

—*Giridhar Naveen Jaded*

Growing divide

If Love is an emotion with a presence,

A feeling beyond an omnipresent existence,

A way of realizing a selfless inner essence,

Given a name, given for reminiscence,

But one that exists in all forms, all relations alike,

To be drawn from, for as long as we like,

A menacing thought though, it irks my conscience,

Why is it that we see Love in compartments?

For its form seems to be a little mangled,

It's reaches curtailed, somewhat entangled,

Reaching only to the select few, privileged,

While thousands yearn in Love, even to be fed,

The need to divide what we have, is a want ancient,

The aftereffects through ages, stark and evident.

—*Giridhar Nitin Jaded*

A worthwhile try

I thought my tries would keep me alive,

I thought my vibes would keep me alive,

I thought my lies would keep me alive

I thought my jibes would keep me alive,

I thought my fantasies would keep me alive,

I thought my confusions would keep me alive

But I think I secretly wished to die,

But not before I had touched the skies,

Not before I had given it a worthwhile try,

Not without feeling Love in all its prime,

Not before I had spread a few smiles,

Not before I had let my words go dry,

Not without few times uber-sensically alive,

Not before I have found a meaning to life.

—*Giridhar Nandan Jaded*

You can

The screen it kept showing a flat line,

Where a zigzag straddled out of line,

Not long ago, just a few seconds ago,

When a trembling voice had meekly said hello,

And now the face it turns pale, yellow,

In a few moments, gone is the halo,

The halo called Life, that breathed in him,

Until it was time for him to cross that line,

The words he said though still hung around,

They simmered in senses without a sound,

Never had his family stood so still, not once,

Let alone in pretense, or lost in deep introspection,

'You saw what I was, you also saw what I wasn't,

You saw what I could, you also saw what I couldn't,

Remember all of that but most of all, remember YOU CAN."

—*Giridhar Deepthi Jaded*

Wait for the turn

In those moments of nothingness,

Where the world is measured in loneliness,

When the coldness inside, it beckons,

And the mind erroneously misfires and reckons,

Visualizing every presence as them demons,

Dictating uncalled for blatant sermons,

Reeling helplessly to those summonses,

Engaging in unscrupulous, uncalled for responses,

Just remember to keep a little of that traction,

For the way out is through the friction,

Between the bouts of doubts in your wailing mind,

And our responses of the frivolous kind,

Soon enough though, there shall be a turn,

Of those invisible whimsical wheels, in the right direction.

—*Giridhar Abhishek Jaded*

Lovely Ms. Air

I have a simple, nimble, humble wish,

My words falling in Love, then planting a kiss,

Onto thin air, in an attempt to coerce,

Her into using her strength, her inner force.

Through which she carries life and all of life's feelings,

Alongside blessings, sighs and other inklings,

To coerce her to carry a few of my words,

Across horizons which I currently traverse,

And to land them as pages that shall be opened,

Looked into, dwelled into, then unraveled,

Into making a meaning one's own, or leading to,

A trip down one's memory lane, ending up smiling too,

On a bookshelf or on a broken windowsill,

Lovely Ms. Air, carry my words if you will?

—*Giridhar Shwetha Jaded*

Old Spice shaving cream

A simple redundant act done every day,

At times has more meaning hidden away,

Known only to the one devotedly following,

A fleeting memory, and try bringing it into the living,

I wonder how many businesses thrive,

When people try to keep memories alive,

For what can be a mere utility, a product,

Can also mean a lot more, in retrospect,

For in a billion acts that we all wade through,

A few habits as well, do sneak through,

A thousand miles away from where it all started,

I still find an Old Spice Shaving cream, packed in red,

What I need is an old-fashioned brush, in white,

To get through that memory trail, feeling alright.

—*Giridhar Avinash Jaded*

At the halfway mark

A wise man in a responsible position,
Whose words carried hopes of a nation,
As millions expected a bit more gumption,
As they listened, ears strained, in anticipation,
Amidst the thick of things, it all feels different,
The banter from outside is almost non-existent,
Yet expectations of fans, aren't they persistent?
Eyes filled in hope, following a sport, pertinent,
For when nations go at one another in a game,
It's not a war, but there's a lot riding, and at fray,
At halfway mark, he said the exact words,
'*We should be alright*' and in plain hindsight,
It seemed more of a question than an answer right,
For there were self-doubts hiding in plain sight,
Seemed more of a self-assurance alright,
Half a battle remained to be fought, standing upright.

—*Giridhar Pratik Jaded*

Back to the front

If fear beckons at you, you stare back,

Even if it isn't in your face, you stare back,

For its way wiser than showing your back,

Hard to get off, once it climbs on your back.

It's a demon best told, coldly to head back,

It doesn't flicker, it excels in the Art of comebacks,

Your eyes shall flicker, when you stare back,

The shivers shall pass, hold on, do not look back,

In time, when fear sees you standing uptight,

Staring at what once looked and seemed fragile,

It will acknowledge seeing you at the battle front,

Hiding a cold shiver inside, it gives a nod, upfront,

Fear has too much pride, won't declare you a victor ever,

It slithers away, finds another victim, until forever.

—*Giridhar Karthik Jaded*

That little note

Beauty has its essence in many ways,

At times in subtle things that faintly hold sway,

Amidst the juggernaut of life that rolls on,

Hobbling along, like a cascading song,

At times, it's the little gestures that steal the heart,

Or memories-golden, from a murkier past,

For in trying to find an essence in the present,

To recreate a soulful and fulfilling experience,

To relive the moment through the same senses,

Yet feeling different, maybe more intense,

Life's a journey that takes us to far off places,

And in those places, seldom seen are the traces,

Of frivolous real-world acts, of trading aces,

A glimpse of a note to myself, written long time back,

Made me see life's beauty again, and I lost track.

—*Giridhar Rashmi Jaded*

Radio silence

A group messenger app it was a boon,
A keyword search, wham, where's the problem?
A bunch of informed people belonged,
To the group about life that stumbled, yet got along,
I like to observe and feel, then to speak,
So, I was a silent member, so to speak,
Of the million messages that were sent,
Few were exchanges, most were forwards, never read,
A question from a beautiful lass, as a profile pic,
Evoked more responses, and lightning quick,
She basked in a moment of glory, only to realize,
She will be gnawed upon, if she just smiled back.
A question about a malfunctioning iPad,
Created a logical ruckus and ideas clashed,
But there was radio silence in an eerie way,
When someone asked, '*how to live life anyway*'.
—*Giridhar Preethi Jaded*

Bring along your bugle

What is it that I really have to offer?

Is it more a thing of mind over matter?

And about those beliefs in us that faintly flutter,

Like droplets from unexpected showers,

For in the depths that we dwell, deep down,

We know what causes a smile, or a frown,

For it's there that we see the solutions,

To life's existent and the made-up confusions.

Yet when it comes to the things that matter,

Do we have a say in everything that occurs?

For if life's a song, bring along your own bugle,

And raise the pitch, till the voice stops that tremble,

That's when you will notice, them heads will crane a little,

Attention not a birthright, its given to those who fight.

—*Giridhar Kashi Nath Jaded*

Contemplating acts

What is it like to live an entire life?

Believing truly, being mean is alright,

And acting as such, for one's own good,

Unraveling tricks, heeding to the fickle moods,

Or with an intent to scale up a ladder,

Even at the cost of ruffling of feathers,

Or transcend a day of gloomy weather,

Onto an unsuspecting soul, who was lost in laughter,

Is there a vibe that falsely casts a spell?

Leading such people to dance to minds-unwell?

And does that spell have an alluring sweep,

Bringing about a rather peaceful sleep?

Are such acts excuses for unfulfilled promises to keep?

Or engraved as right, in hearts black, down so deep?

—*Giridhar Kiran Jaded*

Step-truth

I will speak those very words,
As truth, which you want to hear,
I will hold back my truth for you,
For that fear in your eyes, it comes through.
But what difference does it make,
When you know my words will be fake,
Maybe it's just another give and take,
In your world where it's okay to fake,
Would my words though find a place?
Deep inside you, when reality strikes?
Or will my words be that anesthetic,
Numbing a while, like an analgesic?
What if I uttered utter truth instead?
Would you accept it or shiver in dread?

—*Giridhar Kotish Jaded*

Ain't such a dork?

What if all the Saturdays of our life,

Were to be brought together in a line,

To live a few years filled with Saturdays,

One after another, like wildly spinning blades?

Ever wonder how that would really feel,

A dream come true, too good to be real.

Or a knot in the gut from a hypnotic wheel,

Or a life filled with hope, a newfound zeal,

Would you have a breakfast, a brunch or meal,

How would your life be, how would it really feel?

What would we wait for, day in-day out?

Would we be the same or a different Gould?

I tried to change a calendar, didn't work,

I turned to my mind, it listens, ain't such a dork.

—*Giridhar Aanshi Jaded*

Hang tight

If it is about chasing your dreams,

And about surpassing those realms,

Laid out by the world, layered as cream,

Looking delectable, neat and clean,

Then it doesn't matter what you see,

Its more about what you do and could be,

For beyond what naked eyes can clearly see,

Lay an ocean full of mystic possibilities,

Where one who dives in, feels a rush,

Driven by intent, eking out a firm push,

To those dreams, that must be reached, inch by inch,

Was never meant to be, without a flinching pinch.

Remember those many times where you badly cringed,

Yet days later found yourself on a hopeful brink,

Hang in there if you have a dream, and hang tight,

For there shall be a way, if you have tried alright.

—*Giridhar Ananya Jaded*

Not a straddler

Do not be an urchin, for it slowly devours the seas

Be the coral that keeps many a lives' alive,

Be an orangutan that tends for years,

To her babies till they no longer fear,

Do not be a shark that kills just for fun,

A shark got to eat, but can killing really be fun?

Be a collared Pika who hibernates a lot,

Yet in the spring, lives life a wholesome lot,

Do not be a cuckoo that steals a nest,

Why be the reason for someone else's unrest?

Be a roof even if torn, that gives a shade,

To someone in need, looking for a change,

Be all you can be but don't be a straddler,

Who loiters along like nothing really matters!

—*Giridhar Amit Jaded*

Promising teens

The days you spend in your tumultuous teens,

Wondering how else life could have been,

Let me tell you those will easily be seen,

In future, by you yourself as frivolous worries indeed,

For life then on starts to respectfully treat,

You as an adult, as a grown up indeed.

For being in the teens is a potent pedestal,

From where a launch can be planned, rather powerful,

And if a launch is caught up in hindsight,

There's not much girth in taking that flight,

Hormones or not, learn a lot, have some fun,

But when it's time to make that crazy run,

Make some friends who see you through in silence,

Make some bonds that hold on, are resilient,

Don't be caught up, submerged in just the seas of fun,

Lest you be left with frivolous worries - left alone.

—*Giridhar Deepak Jaded*

What's on your platter?

Appease those minds with the lure,

Appease those minds with the glitter,

Appease those minds with the glamor,

Appease them with a raging fervor,

Instill those minds with an inherent fear,

Instill it for the fear of losing something dear,

Instill it for losing something that they have,

Instill it like a mole that follows till the grave,

Torment those minds with distractions,

Torment them with happiness in fractions,

Torment them bereft of caste, creed or factions,

Torment till those minds start to accept inhibitions,

Appease, Instill, Torment as the three musketeers,

Life does all three, as past liberated souls stand and cheer,

Life's a game and isn't dished out on a platter,

Unto us really, how much of it should we let, matter?

—*Giridhar Prashanth Jaded*

Unseen parody

Hold my hand, I could take you higher,
Play your games, and I shall douse you with fire,
I am that sapphire that transpires,
Into a gem that's shines bright, to inspire.
But if it's my vengeance that you aspire,
Oh I could chase you down to your pyre.
Walk with me if you see some good,
We shall get lost in bliss, in the eerie woods,
Push me back, yeah try all you want,
Can slow me down but stop me you can't.
I sway in my own world, a glimpse of which,
Could enlighten your day, I hope, and wish,
What tomorrow holds is an unseen parody,
Why not try making it a beautiful melody?

—*Giridhar Krishna Jaded*

Labels on Calendars

If a Monday left me wailing,

And a Tuesday left me waiting,

If a Wednesday left me hoping,

And a Thursday left me wanting,

A Friday so dear I can't be sleeping,

Until a weekend had had its beginning,

I wonder if I would really be living,

Or rather spending days waiting?

For the unseen is in no hurry of happening,

What's the point then, in hyperventilating?

If there's girth in patiently waiting,

There's also cowardice in doing nothing,

As I wonder, another Friday slides on over,

A weekend calls on, egging me to stay over.

—*Giridhar Sudha Jaded*

Power of thoughts

A frail-some moment of a plausible act,
Not in the act but just in a thought,
Can at times withhold a larger fight,
Dispelling darkness, bringing about light.
For even a little thought has enough gumption,
To make way, for the unseen redemption,
Of everything that we are, and wish to be,
To turn impossible into, a mere possibility.
A moment of reckoning isn't always an act,
Hold it right there, that's a beautiful fact,
A fact that most battles are won in the mind,
Not outside where half-hearted acts thrive,
Hold on to your whim, hold on to your fantasy,
And live it in the mind till it turns into destiny,
Use the power of thoughts like your alibi,
To surge ahead with intent filled actions aplenty.
—*Giridhar Shobha Jaded*

Find the light

Derailed intentions, they stumbled in the dark,

Deranged actions, they loitered in the back,

Battered emotions, they tried hard to stand,

Fractured notions stood buried in the sand.

A dark cloud of despair hovered above,

A light red sadistic halo, held those clouds,

A nasty odor filled the dampened air,

A hollow tune played hauntingly, out of nowhere,

Gloomy eyes looked around, unsure,

If anything would make a difference, if ever,

And that's when someone in the forlorn crowd,

Picks up a bugle and shouts out aloud,

If we move now, maybe we will find the light,

Less we stay, and fade, toothless, and fade in fright,

And soon enough a few of them hustled,

A sudden rush of warm air in cold hearts, ruffled,

And days went by, then came the whistles,

A belief had found a home, now with pointed bristles.

—*Giridhar Shilpa Jaded*

From the other side

A year ago, he stood right on Wall Street,

Suited up in checks, looking dapper in tweed,

He had pretty much everything a man could need,

Yet he found himself engulfed by greed,

For standing there right between it all, in the middle,

Of the hustle, bustle, fickle, and the brittle,

He still found his feet on the ground,

And dreamt of flying forever around,

The next best thing, a deadly game indeed,

Who defines best, and how much is the need?

He ignored the swollen bills, and the pile of things,

Felt drawn in, kept hanging onto shiny things,

He stands in Wall Street now, holding a placard this time,

Watches the bustle all over again, from the other side.

—*Giridhar Kittu (Pramod) Jaded*

I may never buy a VR

The first time I watched a video on a VR,
I drifted into a third world that seemed very far,
Where my imagination had to take a backseat,
And the world around, started to glisten and blink,
In colors so vivid I felt the blue kiss me,
And I saw a black haze ride graze off on me,
It was as if I was there, as another presence,
Living those moments, feeling the essence,
I tried to connect with my thoughts, but I couldn't,
As hard as I would try, budge they wouldn't,
The colors turned a crimson red all around,
I gasped for a breath, and almost cried out loud,
For the VR it tried to recreate, or to come close,
To my imaginary world that I hold at my chest, even close.

—Giridhar Sunil Jaded

Not counting my miles

These moments of my life that flip by,

With me resembling a stranger, looking by,

Being amazed at the things that transpire

Wondering if this is what I once aspired,

Worrying if I am ahead, or far off behind,

In a jigsaw puzzle residing in my own mind,

For in the maze out there, lies a game,

Addictive like crushing candies, even if lame,

I used to once play that stupid game,

Hell, I even fantasized about a hall of fame,

But then it struck me quick, like a lightning,

There a calm in treading light, in just plainly being,

And to live a little more in the mind, like a homecoming,

And in time, I see the maze turn a straight line,

And I walk along, not counting my miles.

—*Giridhar Mamatha Jaded*

Diabetics of Love

She worked at the bakery in the corner,
Monday to Friday from eight to four,
She could beat the clock if she wished,
That's what people said, called her Ms. Nice,
It wasn't at the bakery that Mr. Brat,
He named himself that, saw her at a park,
She held a baby sheep like her own part,
And that's when he first felt a tiny spark,
Wasn't into sweets, but was rather sweet,
He became a clock all around the week,
He brought a pastry every single day,
A word or two more exchanged every day,
And as their love story started to flourish,
A homeless man got admitted as a diabetic.

—*Giridhar Suresh Jaded*

When mirror flew

She named her son a parrot,

For he spoke so sweet,

He named his Mom a sparrow,

For she sang so mellow,

He brought her a nest,

High up in the mountains,

She gave him a mirror,

A little one, told him it's his future,

He made friends with them foes,

To live in peace, not them chaos,

She pointed the mirror into the sky,

Told him that's where your future lies,

Fly all you can but also try,

To send a bird or two more into the sky,

For there's a bliss in sharing usually unknown,

Until one has had an experience on their own,

And Parrot, he flashed real in the mirror bright,

Flapped his wings, started his ascent into the skies.

—*Giridhar Shashan Jaded*

Blind recluses

The dry leaves on the ground they tell a tale,

Laying crumpled, abandoned, looking pale,

Where once greenery resided amidst them chirps,

A bison now lurks, wailing in uncomfortable burps.

Where once a shade of comfort solemnly resided,

Abandonment and loneliness, has now presided,

Where once three species lived as a family,

Filling days and nights with sounds and activity,

Is now seen a deathly silence that glares,

Back at humanity with red, bloodshot eyes,

For what humanity sought in abundance,

Was a demise of other peaceful existences,

And we as a species excel in the Art of making excuses,

Seeing just fine yet hiding behind blind recluses.

—*Giridhar Sunil Jaded*

A soul's heartburn

If not here, where else would I be,

If not this, what else would I be,

If not now, when shall I turn the key,

If not me, who else is it gonna be,

Aren't these pertinent questions in reality?

Inkling thoughts in all of us, without disparity,

If life is a well-known to-be-lived mystery,

Questions then are apostles, upholding a victory,

A victory of change over a predefined trajectory,

A victory of possibility over a life sedentary,

For without questions how we would then learn,

Be caught up in a mad rush, to just earn?

For when the bones turn into nothing but urn,

It's quite possible a soul might have a heartburn,

It's in the present though that all answers lay,

To what the future protects, neatly tucked away.

—*Giridhar Sharath Jaded*

An unraveling, unique

If all the heartfelt words that made it,

Across emotional barriers, finally nailed it,

Nailed the moment that the feelings got freed,

From being just feelings to shapes indeed,

Like a sweaty bird coming out of the nest,

To flap them wings, let the air do the rest,

Shapes as Art or words on a piece of paper somewhere,

That lay crumpled in a corner elsewhere,

Or typed up in a notepad on a smartphone,

Remains a secret in androids and iPhones,

What if all such scribbled thoughts come out,

Tagged to names, pasted on a wall or read out aloud,

What kind of revelations would come out then?

Would it be more about love or pain written?

I wonder how many likes and shares would erupt,

On an unraveling as powerful as that!

—*Giridhar Rakesh Jaded*

Taking shortcuts

The way of life, taking shortcuts,

Is filled with umpteen thrills, and them little cuts,

That appear one by one on a soul,

Hidden in layers, inside a darker inner core,

They start like mold, unnoticed yet scavenging,

And end up being rather invisible and conniving,

For the lure of getting there soon,

It sets into motion, a soul's impending doom,

But for a heart that marches, hiding behind a bush,

What's a family or a bond or a brood,

It's like drifting down a lovely looking slope,

Not really knowing where it goes,

For every time under the Sun on a mountain,

Might not feel the same, for life's a funny game,

The ride from shortcuts brings about fun, purely from the speed,

Even if a ditch awaits in the end, slimy and filled with grease.

—*Giridhar Praveen Jaded*

Easy to put on

She made herself believe it was Love,

For she wanted her life on the move,

Away from the drudgery that he had left behind,

No stone left unturned, for he left in kind.

She had a choice to then chase a dream,

Or wait in line, be named the top of the cream,

Yet another option was to just let it go,

And to live life, not wanting to play to and fro,

Her frivolous mind it then played a game,

Mixed all her options, gave it to her mind,

And when craving, every morsel is a meal,

The insides though, they slowly start to reveal,

The bruises from the unfelt moments lived,

Start to get darker, decisions when peeved,

If unwanted emotional hurt it keeps adding on,

Onto inner layers easy to put on, hard to get off.

—*Giridhar Vishal Jaded*

Random thoughts

If everything is meant to be temporary,

Why does life, at times feel sedentary?

If everything happens, happens as destiny,

Why then need we create opportunities?

If everything is a means to an end,

What then justifies some acts of violence?

If everything is meant to be an illusion,

Why is there a fulfillment in inventions?

If everything we see is not worth believing,

Is there a fact book full of plain truths, worth knowing?

If everything is meant to eventually be just fine,

Why is there an increase in hatred and crimes?

If everything is meant to just wither away,

How then can we make lives worthy anyway?

—*Giridhar Ravi Jaded*

The power in words

The words 'you will be a great Mom',

To a single Mom contemplating suicide,

The words 'I see something in you',

To someone with a spark, on the verge of giving up,

The words 'you are on the right track',

To someone going through a lot of strife,

The words 'we will make it through',

In a bond that's riding some rough waves,

The words 'good is just around the corner',

To someone reeling under a natural disaster,

The words 'I will be there for you',

To someone trying to see loneliness through,

Little pockets of heartfelt words, of compassion in life,

Make a world of difference, when timed right.

—*Giridhar Gokul Jaded*

A Happy Birthday

The faces, looked glorified in candlelight,

The eyes, they glistened with hope and life,

The smiles, they welcomed everyone alike,

The laughter, it froze a few moments in time,

These emotions, they belonged to little kids,

Who had been abandoned adrift, like things,

Some had seen a faint glimpse of their Mom,

While some wore a face rigid and forlorn,

For most of the time, but not this evening,

They had company, to imagine a new beginning,

And today was special, it was a group birthday,

Of all the kids who had just a lot of time, to play,

In that one evening, many of those little kids,

Garnered strength, to smile on for a few more weeks.

—*Giridhar Prashanth Jaded*

Society

We throw open a Pandora's box in vanity,

Sprinkling in sectors and statuses for variety,

Add a little more of a perplexing hierarchy,

For some of us devour on notions of anarchy,

Grind in some rules, regulations, some disparity,

Create a divide between elite and the ordinary,

Throw in a few shams as opportunities,

Mix it with an ounce of well-directed exclusivity,

Create a wave for masses to nod helplessly,

Name it a revolution, justifying that profanity,

Dispel notions on possibility, via falsified victories,

Try and hold peace with the minds, on the verge of insanity,

A creation of humanity, one filled with mystery,

Is what we all proudly live in, a Society.

—Giridhar Kiran Jaded

She's alright

She walked in shadows no one else did,
She hid in darker places like no one else hid,
For what she had seen as a little kid,
It messed up her mind, like hell it did.
And her concept of trust was shattered,
By the very gentlemen who she thought, mattered,
Only difference was, they were not gentle,
Rather psychotics, and wrong-wired mortals,
The very hands meant to care, and to protect,
Were used to quell a blooming flower's self-respect,
Well before it started to even blossom,
Leaving scars and a heart badly broken.
Those sleepless nights crouched in her bed,
For decades, often sweating out with dread,
Now finally lay rested, for she now has a plan,
To leave such men behind, as a morbid clan,
She walks along, now having left behind,
The darker men in shadows, she's alright.

—*Giridhar Sandeep Jaded*

Sunset or her?

As the wind settled and her face cleared,

Her tresses fluttered and gently wavered,

From left to right they danced like dew drunk leaves,

Basking under an artificial sprinkle and that breeze,

As they rested, she nonchalantly looked,

At me with eyes that meant, I had been missed,

And in that moment, I felt a gush of wind,

And a wave of the unknown, in an uprising,

Nature has its ways to make the hearts sway,

A drizzle began, driving the sordid heat away,

A pair of lucky droplets found their place,

Damn, the lucky retards landed right on her face.

And that's when I noticed a beautiful sunset behind,

And then at her, found my answer, and smiled.

—*Giridhar Vinayak Jaded*

At the gates

Those steely eyes that stare ahead,

Standing at another nation's gates,

Stared back with fiery eyes, nothing to hide,

From the soldiers on the other side,

I wonder if between the larger divide,

Life sometimes finds a way to override,

And create moments that dispel some notions,

Through moments of heartfelt human emotions,

Is there a camaraderie in a military routine?

Knowing that a presence on the other side,

Is also nothing but the humankind,

Unaware yet aware, caught up in a bind,

Through the rules written, by a hierarchy,

Build on foundations driven by anarchy,

Is there an exchange of some form of a pleasantry?

Either for gallantry or in times of festivities?

With an understanding that when the time comes,

Those very hands will be holding heavy metal, as guns?

—*Giridhar Ramakrishna Jaded*

Starkness, even in good

A morning time coffee,

A lighthearted movie,

A comforting soul as my company,

And lighthearted camaraderie,

A picture perfect 4K TV,

Internet streaming easy and breezy?

Or

A morning walk on the beach,

A margarita, a tinge of peach,

Just the waves and winds in reach,

A jovial banter, awkwardness breached,

A picture-perfect sunset,

A day with not much else, to repent?

—*Giridhar Daniel Jaded*

Breezy belief

There's a sense of calm in believing,
In knowing something worth knowing,
About oneself, something exhilarating,
And in the act of patiently waiting,
For there's no sin in not knowing,
Or in knowing what's worth knowing,
As long as what you really believe in,
Is something good and in a way, fulfilling.
The whims and fallacies from outside,
Shall one day cease, and maybe subside,
Leaving a calm inside your invigorated mind,
If your belief indeed, heartfelt and worthwhile,
I feel such a breeze every time that I believe,
And yet the future beckons, I ain't in no hurry to leave.

—*Giridhar Vikas Jaded*

My silly world

What makes me, me is just me,

Yet there's a nimble need to be,

Be what the world expects me to be,

Doesn't matter if I clearly see,

The path that they carved out for me,

For my mind is a world itself, quite silly,

Where there's more of those possibilities,

Of fine tuning even hideous opportunities,

For it's in the act of truly believing,

There lies a beautiful insight, worth unraveling,

Possibilities that once existed just as dreams,

Can be brought to the fore in real life, as parallel realms,

I have listened till now, have walked your path,

I want to now choose my own walks in the park,

I will continue believing to no end,

And let the world find its own means to be end.

—*Giridhar Swaminath Jaded*

If I could, you could too

I have loitered in those dark places often,
Where laziness engulfed me like a demon,
And I felt like a flagpole amidst a big rubble,
Feeling my presence, yet in a way feeling nimble.
I have uprooted those wires and traveled far,
Many a times, yet fallen back on the radar,
I guess I see fitness as not belonging too far,
It's to be kept near, like a never-ending well-fought war.
And it feels like a war only until a point,
After which it sticks around, kinda conjoined,
I ain't a fitness beast but I do eat my feast,
From beautiful walks or runs, or a pull ups heist,
Give up not until you have broken a sweat,
In the morning Sun or in front of your closet,
Or at a gym some place or your own garage,
Fitness is a mystery to be solved, more so a mirage,
If you are loitering right now, worry not,
Take a first step and leave the results, like worries to rot.

—*Giridhar Vineet Jaded*

Across the finish line

Woke up this morning, feeling quite ok,
Had an obstacle race to start and finish, then come back ok,
It started off well under the summer heat,
I could almost hear a passerby's heartbeat,
Lost my earphones right before the start,
Oopsie moment, there was no looking back,
Didn't have my upbeat songs for company
Yet had the presence of Spartans aplenty,
Second time lesson learnt, hydrating well,
Before a race is basic, also very crucial,
A few cramps meant I had to buckle up,
If I had to trod on until the victory lap,
Had known this would be mind over body,
One more medal to a kitty I call my booty.

—*Giridhar Amruth Jaded*

Written on June 22, 2019 after finishing Spartan
Sprint Race at ATT Stadium, Dallas, Texas.

Burden called perceptions

The perceptions we make about a country,

Does it consider an entire story?

Or rather glimpses of what's soon to be history,

Planned in the present, planted for future-skillfully?

For the portraits we see as getting painted,

Are in a way disoriented, oftentimes dissipated,

For what transpires in an entire nation,

Is far beyond anyone's imagination,

An inspiration here, a tragedy there,

A miracle here, a budding revolution there,

A communion here, a separation there,

A mandate lifted here, a rule mended there,

Aren't people just people, just the ways different,

Perceptions when left buried, revelations do happen.

—*Giridhar Vinit Jaded*

Not choosing sides

Do not push me to choose one side,

For I don't relate to the path you ride,

In a battle created not on its own,

But only by you in your mind, so torn,

And when I don't feel a part of your fight,

What difference if I hold a pen or a knife,

To you that is, for me I will find my bliss,

And to your games, I will blow a goodbye kiss.

It's not the trading of blows that matters,

It's the one flying higher, when it matters,

Would be a cardinal sin, counting me weak,

I would rather wipe tears, but I could make you weep

But you know what, I have promises to keep,

Holler at me once you know what you really seek.

—Giridhar Prabhu Jaded

I race, tomorrow

Tomorrow is the day I shall race,

Again, this time with a new grace,

For the last time I was in a race,

Fear and I had come face to face,

And I had stood tall till the end,

I was stubborn, not willing to give in, to bend,

And I shall climb, run, jump yet again,

Even feel those sweet, gentle, nimble pains,

But between all this, I shall also have fun,

As I challenge myself, whilst on the run,

What started as a test drive, is now a commute,

The realizations that dawn - fierce, as well astute,

I shall do my best, to cross the finish line,

It's a race I do without counting them miles.

—*Giridhar Shivayogi Jaded*

Written on June 21, 2019 on the evening before Spartan
Sprint Race at ATT Stadium, Dallas, Texas.

Haystack in my shoe

The haystack that had stuck into my shoes,
From what I think was roughly three years ago,
It's just a haystack yet it bounces and packs,
A punch through lovely memories of the past,
With a few laughs and also the scares that we had,
Seems long back, but the relapse ain't that bad,
I stare at its presence from where it stands,
A thousand miles away from the white sands,
Where it once looked lush green and even glossy,
Now a pale yellow, drawing me back in history,
A minuscule existence, yet an abundant presence,
The haystack leaves a message, one of essence,
Is it an existence we seek or life's abundance?
It is excellence we seek or merely being a presence?
—*Giridhar Ghanshyam Jaded*

Ain't bad at all

I have felt this before and I feel it again,
There's a palace built for all, with unwelcome pain,
I have said this before and I say this again,
Life isn't just about what we grab, what we gain,
For it's in the see, wish, want, snatch-chain,
That life gets caught, and oftentimes in vain.
For what can justify inflicting a known pain,
Knowing very well there's hurt later to gain,
For what can justify showing steely eyes,
While speaking words that crumble, every line?
For what can justify an obnoxious victory-grin,
With ice standing on, cracked and treacherously thin?
Why not make it a win-win for one and all,
Be kind, see it come back, ain't bad after all.
—*Giridhar Shrinivas Jaded*

Hello of the other side

A wise person, too wise for one's own age,
Once asked me a simple question unique,
'What do I expect from my readers?'
Ooo it was a question for the hooters,
Me being myself took the question apart,
And instead revealed a wish from my heart,
Which went to everyone reading my Art,
Playing an inseparable and soulful part,
Of my journey to find meaning in words,
That I hope act bolder, more than swords,
And my simple wish is just that, one day,
You shall proudly hold a book I wrote away,
And in those moments, you feel drifting away,
I shall glide by, say hello, smile and fade away.
—*Giridhar Sumit Jaded*

Hypocrisy meter

In a world full of glaring truths,

I wonder how come the hypocrites' rule,

For isn't there a device ever made,

That could line us all up, on a common scale,

A scale of hypocrisy standing tall,

Against which we all measure our fall,

For in a way we all have, maybe once,

Danced on a buzz, hypocrisy induced,

To what extent is altogether a different question,

Might need a far deeper contemplation,

Acceptance is a beginning, I am there,

From where I can see the rising air,

All I wish is that I shall forever hold,

A lower rung on hypocrisy scale, all life long.

—*Giridhar Sambit Jaded*

Be by my right

I have never let you out of sight,

But now I am keeping you to my right,

And not the usual, front of my eyes,

For I now have to head on, into a fight,

Where there's a lot wrong, and very less right,

When I crank on my V8 and start to glide,

Make sure you are in my best possible right,

For when those horses listen to my need,

And rise up to the occasion, like a common creed,

They pummel along, seemingly in no mood to heed,

And in a way, that's exactly what I need,

For I shall pull a surprise move, one with speed,

And lend a part of me, to the ones in need,

Or to those who just feel a need to be freed.

—*Giridhar Venugopal Jaded*

The walks back from work

In times when there's not much to do,
I think I know a simple plan, to sail through,
To watch people heading back from work,
And see time while away, rather quick,
For seeing those faces, and the traces,
Of mannerisms and the different paces,
Time slips away for a while into spaces,
Trying to gauge the vibes on those faces,
A hurried walk with a worried look,
A wayward walk, in a cell phone - lost,
A careless sprint, also on a shortcut,
A thoughtful walk, about the work that's left,
A glance at a watch for an evening plan to heed,
A glance at the clouds, less it rains with greed,
Vivid hues of life seen on different days,
Even the same person dispelling vibes, in different ways.

—*Giridhar Shivanand Jaded*

I ain't no Painter

If the world was my canvas, on a compass,
What coordinates, would I then trespass?
Would I paint it all in my favorite color?
Or let the not so favorite ones also appear?
To transcend all the invisible pixels in a way,
That would make colors join hands and play?
What brush would I use, I start to ponder?
For that determines strokes that shall appear,
A thin one for sheer elegance portrayed,
Or a thick one for immense girth portrayed?
As I wonder, I start to feel a silent shiver,
It says from within *'You ain't no Painter'*.
I nod, smile, agree but I would like to try,
To fill the canvas with words that could fly.

—*Giridhar Santosh Jaded*

That one song?

Is there a song ever written?
And sung like it just belonged,
To that one feeling and just one at that,
A feeling of a tingling positive vibe?
For even the most hopeful of songs,
That make our hearts sing along,
Most times they do, but there are also times,
When the same song feels like a silent mime.
For then, if there were such a song,
Why would we have a playlist our own?
Juggling between moods like guitar strings,
Swinging between songs like chimpanzees?
If I find it, I will let you know, and you do too,
One day all playlists shall have that one song to listen to.

—*Giridhar Ruel Jaded*

If I were a wallet

If I were a wallet, whose company would I adorn,

Would it be a celebrity, rich and well known?

Or an average Joe fighting for his daily food?

Or be disowned, from someone adopting sainthood,

Would I adorn someone a spendthrift?

Or someone elegant, caring, as if I were a gift,

Or someone who would often keep me hidden,

And lie plainly about me and my existence?

Would I be a cause for my owner's worry?

Or an answer to solve all the mysteries?

Would I be just a plain status symbol?

Or rather an exhibition of imperialism?

I would cling onto that one person maybe,

Who wouldn't hold me too close, not too far,

Hold me respectfully yet not be driven ajar.

—*Giridhar Karthik Jaded*

What's your trade?

What do you call a missing spade?
In an eclectic deck of cards in red,
Would a game of cards still feel the same?
Or would you pacify your mind? lame.
For even if a play is sitting so high,
On a hundredth-floor pool, a view to drool,
A game of cards would it be the same,
Despite all the money, glory and the fame?
For in a simple act of being a spade,
A spade holds its own in its tirade,
And requests a respect it truly deserves,
For it upholds what it wishes to preserve,
Do you have your deck, if so what's your spade?
What's your mastery, what's your trade?

—*Giridhar Pramod Jaded*

A walk on the mountains

Would you walk with me on the mountains?
And look down upon freshwater fountains,
And gaze into the skies, beautiful and blue,
Breathing an air of calm, afresh anew?
For what I like to do while we are up there,
To my weird mind, feels just reasonably fair
For when we are up there, feeling the air,
There shall be an unraveling, in what I shall say,
For what I seek is a few moments we shall miss,
In our future, to be looked back as moments of pure bliss,
For a conversation out there in the mountains,
Is better than half-hearted day to day interactions,
For when the words do find their way right,
There's a moment where we internally feel alright.

—*Giridhar Shyam Jaded*

Answers to find

Is it all about what we really think,

Or more so about whether we even think?

Is it all about what we really do,

Or more so about what we don't?

Is it all about how we really behave,

Or more so about the number of times we cave?

Is it all about what we really wear,

Or more about what we can carry with flair?

Is it all about what we really own,

Or more so about what we know as our own?

Is it all about the places to which we travel,

Or more about finding that inner tranquil?

Is it all so mixed up as it really seems,

Or more about yanking open the doors to the right realms?

—*Giridhar Bapugowda Jaded*

Predator and prey

Do you want to play predator and prey?

With someone who hasn't learnt giving away.

Would you risk it all to maybe carry away?

A probable cause, in your fantasy parade?

Where only those frivolous, untowardly acts rule,

Dancing to negativity like drunken mules,

I see the nod of air, of affirmation you gave,

Did you even notice I own my own conclave?

Of experiences, in dealing with ones like you,

Who act timid in a way it really seems true?

But trust me I have it sorted, all the way through,

Even before you thought of landing your first blow,

Now I look at you and wonder, is it needed though?

You looked beaten from the beginning, now even more.

—*Giridhar Vijay Jaded*

Hardwired

He was like a rustic pumice stone,

Stranded, awaiting something, alone,

Alone not because he didn't have one to call his own,

Rather from the choices, that had now become,

A part of his own, in ways hard to now untwine,

From his senses to the bottom of his spine,

He had lived a life on his own trivial terms,

Breaking rules like a pecker pecking on worms,

He wronged the right, wiped it, called it a clean slate,

Then sprinkled it with greed, envy, some conniving mates,

They acted like adrenaline for his fanatic traits,

Until he had forgotten, what he had at stake,

And by now he stood wealthy but weary and tired,

Wondering if it was him that did all this, or was he hardwired?

—*Giridhar Adarsh Jaded*

Weird-some beast

I got to see what I was meant to see,

And it was enough, had nothing more to see,

For what I saw in those little glimpses,

Took me back in time, to see myself in braces,

Bouncing off aces hurled at me, at insane paces,

And to those lowly moments of forgetful existence,

What it seemed, wasn't what it later became,

Or was it the same, maybe I was blind, insane?

But now I have seen beyond those smiles,

Hidden beneath ruffled feathers, your every disguise,

And you think you had me wrapped up in a foil,

Ready to be grilled, deep fried in heated oil,

Sad enough for you, I am a weird-some beast,

I choose the places where I sit and savor my feasts.

—*Giridhar Rajani Jaded*

Mrs. Grumpy and Mr. Happy

As her little dog Beaver played in a yard,

Mrs. Grumpy drifted into memories not so old,

When Beaver was a threat to the outer world,

On a waitlist to be put down, file shut and close.

He had acted as if bitten by an angry bird,

Threw tantrums in rage, acted rather weird,

And in his rage, he had jumped at Mr. Happy,

Who got shit-scared, cried for a nappy,

He got Beaver into a place of utter doom,

Where animals wished they could have spoken,

For little Beaver as a pup, had seen an accident,

Where a mirror was a cause, and a death was imminent,

Left a scar on the little one's conscience,

To act in defense, aggressively and unusually different,

Seeing a mirror unleashed his inner terror,

Mrs. Grumpy, ever so beautiful, now lives without mirrors.

—*Giridhar Hanumanthappa Jaded*

Gallant acts

What if I woke up one day totally blind?

Or open my eyes, to see an amputated leg,

Or have a gash, running across on my chest,

From a shrapnel that pierced the sturdy vest,

Or spend a few days staring at obscurity,

Felling pride as well as uncalled for empathy,

For the act I engaged in, barging right in,

Was the right thing to do, amidst all the firing,

A mere contemplation of it all, it evokes a fright,

Spare a thought for the ones who walk in and fight,

For deep inside, they as well have a beating heart,

It beats on a higher wavelength, and stands apart,

Words fall short to honor some gallant acts in life,

Respect shown often, in everyday life, just feels right.

—*Giridhar Rachna Jaded*

A two-way breeze

A half-savored glass of Kentucky bourbon,
Untouched, glistening since the weekend,
Winks at me like a flirt, beckons at my wits,
From where it was left at 4am, on that windowsill.
I let it sit there for I do like it's glare,
To see the days flip by, and its lure gets rare,
For in the moments of abstinence as well,
Lay an Art, that we seldom comprehend,
I do wonder how the same glistening glass,
Feels like a Mademoiselle, eclectic in class,
In those moments spent taking it light,
Yet seems a distant stranger, other times,
I sit and wonder if life's a two-way breeze,
Making us feel the opposites, with ease.

—*Giridhar Pavitra Jaded*

Life, a parody unique

What is, today-will one day be long gone,

Swept away under those sands of time,

Works like clockwork does life, encapsulates us humans,

And more masses, that we call as generations.

Time, it rolls by like a raging bull,

To it, there's no such phase as a lull,

For what it envisions is a spectacular show called life,

Where billions of actors live, try, smile and cry.

What's left behind is probably just lessons,

Passed on over never ending progressions,

A revelation unique, rising to the spotlight,

A feeling unique, shared with someone right,

Life is indeed a mesmerizing parody unique,

Where some days seem a straight line, some oblique.

The newness in things is a beautiful thing,

A mesmerizing parody, this act called living.

—*Giridhar Praful Jaded*

To another planet?

Where will all the seagulls fly to,

When the oceans are no longer a beautiful blue?

Where will all the blue whales go,

When their lives versus medicines sees life being let go?

Where will all the primate chimps go,

When there are no trees to call their woods?

Where will all the collared Pika go,

When temperatures are constantly on the move?

Where will the cute little Penguins go,

If arctic ice weakens, and can no longer hold?

Where will all the Dolphins play,

If the seas are poisoned all the way?

Where will all the resilient Camels go?

When the oases in deserts dry all the way through?

Where do you think Humanity will escape and go?

Maybe to another planet, after having seen Earth through?

—*Giridhar Harsh Jaded*

Back, behind

It wasn't the first time he had laid his hands,

Holding by the scruff those empty pangs,

That acted inside him not on his own behalf,

Rather pulled by strings, emanating from the dark.

He had known this presence all along,

Had taken lonesome walks, listening to songs

He had held a string and walked in the dark,

Often found himself back again at the start,

At times the walks ended up in a scar,

Yet he went in, for he was a monster when at war.

He lured the wary demon, learned a trick to finally fool,

It was wary from its sumptuous serving of souls,

A rope tied on his waist, he now drags it on,

As the battered demon agonizingly cries on.

—*Giridhar Viaan Jaded*

Days of the week

Was there a thought behind naming the days?

As Sunday's Monday's or Tuesday's,

Was there a concept behind the names?

To flaunt them together, yet unique in a way?

Or was it just a logical representation,

To dissect equal time, which we all have been given?

Was there a story attached to the days?

From pages of history, or from sages and their tales?

Were they laid out with this intent, the first time,

That made sense back then, but we forgot in time,

Or were they laid out, just the way they now feel?

Like a noisy spoke on a worn out, yet functional wheel?

I sit here and wonder on a Monday morning,

Let me ask google, maybe there's some hidden reasoning.

—Giridhar Krustappa Jaded

Till death do us apart

I have a companion, in a way a soul mate,
Not a chosen one, forced upon by fate,
I lived with him like his shadowy little slave,
And I wondered if he shall follow me to my grave?
With time though, I have worked out my peace,
With its existence, in almost my every inch,
At times, I feel myself wake up, gasping for breath,
Even when wide awake, in broad daylight,
But then I know it's soon gonna be alright,
Am gonna use the discomfort, to set things right.
For a part of me is now a Pain magnet,
It thrives in crevices, corners and in darker closets,
I have found a way to hoist him up high,
And walk along, not letting him cloud my dreamy eyes.

—*Giridhar Deviramma Jaded*

A restless ramble

Drifting between the clouds, I was once,

Caught up in a soulful and hypnotic trance,

A sense of calm resided in the air around,

The colors seemed vibrant, but not too loud,

I shuddered at the thought of seeing an end,

To this feeling of gliding, without being sent,

On chores after chores from the ways of life,

That cling around like spider webs, tall and wide,

And then I felt a welcome sprinkle of cold water,

Onto my face, and in turn created a flutter,

In my heart, from feeling a unending still,

Of a calm that ended, but left a pack of refills,

Of hope, that I gasp on every now and then,

When restless a little, which is quite often.

—*Giridhar Kashibai Jaded*

Fair or unfair?

In those far corners of the world out of sight,

Where everything 's painted in beautiful Snow White,

And there's that stillness in the views, from a lack of life,

It engulfs the air, and an eerie silence resides,

Where the winds howl, like menacing wolves,

Where being at zero, is still a spring of sorts,

Sending chills down the spines, for the ones alive,

I wonder if a certain type would could still survive,

That type of people, are the ones hardened by life,

To an extent that only coldness now presides,

Deep inside a dark heart that still beats alright,

But has lost its spark, to the hurt and strife,

If a cold heart like that would venture there,

What outcome would it be? Fair or unfair?

Seekers of the primitive life, what's on your mind?

Would you care dispel your thoughts, to the humankind?

—*Giridhar Manohar Jaded*

Leap off your fence

Those seemingly small steps that we take,

Inch by inch towards a future at stake,

Seemingly slower than a snail, truth be told,

But there's victory for a heart, that knows to hold.

And hold tight, to what it really believes,

In a world its own, where a dream was conceived,

And like with human life, every birth has its worth,

In nurturing those dreams, is the lesson from Mother Earth.

Being stranded at times, is a feeling temporary,

Listen to your pulse, does it seem sedentary?

Knowing now, look ahead and make that irksome start,

Grit your teeth, if you are headed down the right track,

Then look down again and give it your best walk,

And live a few days believing everything else is dark,

Not far ahead, you will see a scary trench,

And a belief that shall let you leap off your fence.

—*Giridhar Padma Jaded*

Virtual Primes

It's a talk of the folklore, and a fact well known,

That every successful sportsman has had a prime,

In which, statistics and history got tossed around,

Toyed with, like pellets cleared off the ground.

Their prime was the time they really shined,

Dispelling impossibilities as a demon with faces-forlorn,

For in those moments they had taken a pledge,

To ignore sleep, pain, even emotions being on edge,

To then be able to leave a crowd mesmerized to no end,

For when inspiration gets mixed with a deadly desire,

Supported ably by society and the infrastructure,

These sportsmen did what they do best, be livewires,

Believing truly, not reaping a prime-akin to lighting self-pyres,

We often follow sports with passion, see sportsmen as demi-gods,

But turn off the encapsulating screens, we tend to behave rather odd,

If wasting away one's prime is indeed an unforgiving crime,

Why then are students burdened by loans, in their prime?

—*Giridhar Linganagouda Jaded*

www.ingramcontent.com/pod-product-compliance
Lightning Source LLC
Chambersburg PA
CBHW020407150626
46554CB00012B/400